Thomas I. Durant.
11/23-'68

The SHENANDOAH towing prisoners from three burning whaling vessels in Behring's Straits, June 25, 1865.

THE SHENANDOAH;

OR THE

LAST CONFEDERATE CRUISER.

BY

CORNELIUS E. HUNT,

(ONE OF HER OFFICERS).

NEW YORK:
G. W. CARLETON, & CO. PUBLISHERS.
LONDON: S. LOW, SON, & CO.
MDCCCLXVII.

CONTENTS.

CHAPTER I.

CHAPTER II.

CHAPTER III.

CHAPTER IV.

CHAPTER V.

CHAPTER VI.

CHAPTER VII.

CHAPTER VIII.

CHAPTER IX.

CHAPTER X.

THE SHENANDOAH;

OR THE

LAST CONFEDERATE CRUISER.

CHAPTER I.

FROM LONDON TO MADEIRA.

THE Southern Confederacy exists only in the past. The gallant armies which so long resisted the overpowering odds with which they had to contend, are broken and scattered, and for the most part have returned to the pursuits of peace; its Chief languishes, a prisoner of State in a military fortress, and its little navy has ceased to inspire with terror the people of the United States "who go down to the sea in ships, and do business in the great waters."

It came to pass that I was one of the few who witnessed the last descending glory of this attempted Republic, projected by men who considered that the only true and natural foundation of society was "the wants and fears of individuals," but which was decided adversely to *their* interpretation of that natural law, by the God of battles.

What I may have to relate in the succeeding pages is simply the plain, unvarnished narrative — a transcript of the log, if you please — of a sailor, who entered the service of the Confederate States, because he was "to the manor born," and felt in honor bound to follow the fortunes of his State, and who was among the last to turn sorrowfully away from a cause which had no longer a flag to defend, or a Government to save its adherents on the seas from the stigma of piracy.

On Saturday, the 7th of October 1864, the English steamer, "Sea King," left her moorings in London, having cleared for Bombay or any other port in the East Indies, on a voyage not to exceed two years. She was a long, rakish vessel of seven hundred and ninety tons register, with an auxiliary engine of two hundred and twenty nominal horse-power, with which she was capable of steaming ten knots an hour. She was the handiwork of Stevens and Son, the celebrated builders on the river Clyde, in Scotland, and had been launched the preceding year, after which she had made one voyage to New Zealand as a transport for British troops.

On this, her first voyage, she proved herself one of the fastest sailers afloat, her log showing at times over three hundred and twenty miles in twenty-four hours. Such a vessel, with such a prestige, was not likely to escape the notice of the Confederate agents in England, who were on the lookout for suitable craft for privateering purposes, and quietly, so quietly in fact, that except those immediately connected with the transaction, no one was aware of it, this splendid ship was sold to the Confederacy, and lay in the basin taking in coal and provisions sufficient for a twelve month's cruise, without awakening a suspicion in official circles, or even in the mind of the public as to her ultimate destination, or the important part she was to play in the great drama of the American civil war.

When everything was arranged, the Sea King hauled out of the basin, and proceeded to sea under the command of Captain Corbet, an English ship-master, and flying the English flag.

She carried two twelve pounders, such as are usually mounted upon an East Indiaman of her size, and, in brief, so well had the whole affair been managed, that there was nothing in her departure to excite even passing attention. It was only an ordinary vessel setting sail upon an ordinary voyage.

She was scarcely clear of the ground, however, when a telegram was flashed to Liverpool, advising the Confederate agent at that port, that the first part of the great programme had been accurately performed, and about eight o'clock the same evening, a mysterious individual was flitting from place to place in that city, advising certain other persons that the moment they had been so anxiously awaiting for some weeks had arrived; and an hour later, from hotels, boarding-houses, and apartments pretending and unpretending, issued forth a score or more of gentlemen, natives of the sunny South, who had staked life and fortune on the hazard of a desperate game, and took their solitary way towards the landing stage where a steam tug was in waiting to convey them on board the steamer Laurel.

These persons were the officers of the Confederate cruiser Shenandoah, into which the Sea King was to be transformed a few days later at the Island of Madeira, and the steamer Laurel contained her armament and crew, and was to meet her there, although ostensibly bound to Nassau or Havana, with supplies for the Confederate Government.

The Laurel was commanded by Lieutenant Ramsey, and although a Confederate vessel, she flew the English flag.

Our baggage had all been previously sent on board packed in dry goods boxes marked with a diamond and a number above it, by which each officer was known, and at the moment of departure every one was furnished with a receipt, of which the following, except the name (in all cases fictitious) is a copy.

Received from Mr. Elias Smith, thirty-two pounds, for his passage in the cabin of Steamer Laurel, from this port to Havana.

£32. HENRY LAFONE.

It was a chilly October evening, with a heavy mist rendering everything half invisible at a distance of a dozen paces, when after receiving the above document, I sallied forth from my Liverpool lodgings, conscious that at last I was setting out upon the adventurous career for which I had so long been preparing.

No one unless he has stood in a similar place can appreciate the crowd of emotions that whirled through my mind. I was about to join, clandestinely, a vessel commissioned by a Government still in embryo, but which I had sworn to support, to cruise against the commerce of another Government which still claimed me as its liege subject. If the cause I upheld was successful, there was wealth, fame, and glory, to be earned; if it failed, a felon's doom impended over me and my associates; but I was too young and hopeful to long contemplate the dark side of the case; the ship I was to join was afloat; the ocean was before us, and, sailor-like, I was content to put my trust in Providence, Neptune, and the Southern Confederacy.

It was curious, too, as I plodded my solitary way down the wet, slippery street, to see other men accoutred like myself, and bound as I well knew upon the same mission, without venturing to exchange with them a word of greeting, but the injunctions of secrecy were peremptory and too much was at stake for orders to be lightly disregarded.

We were obliged to be thus secret in our movements, to avoid being detected by some of the numerous spies employed by the United States Consul at Liverpool, to watch the movements of the Confederates in that city, and prevent if possible the shipment of munitions of war or the fitting out of vessels in the Southern interest; consequently the Laurel's passengers affected to be entire strangers to each other and avoided all appearance of concert of action until they were safe on board. This was accomplished before midnight, and having shown our receipts, we were conducted to our state-rooms and berths, and at 4 A. M., proceeded to sea under steam.

After passing Holyhead and getting fairly outside, all restraint was thrown off, and we warmly congratulated Captain Ramsey upon the admirable manner in which he had succeeded in eluding the lynx eyes of Uncle Sam's men, and getting to sea with the armament to equip, and the officers to take charge of, our new cruiser.

It was, upon the whole, a merry company that assembled in the cabins of the Laurel that memorable Sunday morning. There were some faces upon which the shadow of parting from loved ones still lingered, and some heavy hearts, I doubt not, were concealed under a gay exterior, but there was so much that was alluring in the wild romance of the life before us, such a wide range for hope, so many probabilities in our favor, that care, sorrow, and anxiety drifted pretty rapidly to leeward, and with the first splicing of the main brace disappeared.

Among our passengers were several old Confederate States Navy officers, who had served on board the Sumter, Alabama, and Georgia, and of course they had much to tell us of their experience, and our voyage was enlivened by many a yarn, such as none but an old cruiser can spin, and with excellent accommodations, a well-appointed table, and other creature comforts unnecessary to specify more particularly, we succeeded in enjoying ourselves to the utmost.

On the morning of the sixth day out from Liverpool, we sighted the Island of Madeira, and before noon dropped anchor in the harbor of Funchal.

CHAPTER II.

FROM MADEIRA TO THE "LINE."

AFTER circumnavigating the globe, I have no hesitation in saying that Funchal is one of the most beautiful and salubrious places it was ever my good fortune to visit, although my opportunities for observation were limited to spy-glass explorations, as we dared not leave the vessel for fear of awakening suspicion as to our true character.

The city has several buildings of considerable architectural pretensions. One in particular, of which we had a fine view from the harbor, is known as Mount Church, and occupies the summit of a bold bluff several thousand feet above the level of the sea, from which its two tall, white towers stand out in bold relief against this almost cloudless sky. The church is reached by a road that zigzags up the bluff a distance of nearly four miles, — a by no means easy pedestrian excursion, and is generally performed on horseback, but the return trip to town is usually made upon sleds, at the invigorating rate of some twenty miles an hour. To a native of the Northern States this would be refreshingly suggestive of the boyish pastime of coasting; and some idea of the steepness of the declivity may be gathered by the rate of speed at which, as I have stated, the Madeira sleds glide down the rocky pathway, which is paved with smooth, round stone.

Among the other public edifices, I may mention the Blind Asylum, where some exquisite artificial flowers are manufactured from feathers, by the young girls, its inmates, and also baskets of every shape and description, pretty ornamental things in their way, which are disposed of to the ships visiting the port, for the benefit of the Institution.

The fortress commanding the harbor has been hewn out of the natural rock, and is a most formidable structure, a sort of pocket edition of Gibraltar, in fact, and, thoroughly armed and garrisoned, would be an ugly place to carry by assault.

After remaining at anchor for two days we began to feel some uneasiness in regard to the Sea King, as sufficient time had elapsed to enable her to make the run, but we were not fated to be kept long in suspense. On the evening of the third day the absentee made her appearance and commenced signalling, but as it was contrary to rules to leave the harbor after dark, we perforce remained where we were until morning, when, having received permission from the authorities on shore, we stood out to meet her.

Although there was a fresh breeze blowing at the time, we had a full head of steam on, and as we neared her, we signalled her to round the Desertas, a barren, rocky island, lying near Madeira, and proceeded on towards the place of rendezvous, the Sea King following in our wake.

In about three hours we succeeded in rounding the island, and had the good fortune to find an excellent place for discharging our armament and ammunition, from the Laurel to her consort. Everything was auspicious for the work before us. Scarce a breath of air coquetted with the idle sails, and the ocean around us was as smooth as a mill-pond. But moments were precious; the power against which we were about to commence hostilities was active and vigilant; its iron-clad floating fortresses ploughed the sea in every direction, and some such unwelcome visitor might disturb us at our work at any moment; consequently all felt the necessity of rapidly discharging the important duty that devolved upon us.

Tackles were at once got aloft on both vessels, and we commenced operations by first transferring from the Laurel to the Sea King the heavy guns. This was the most difficult part of our labor; indeed the rest was comparatively easy. Both officers and men worked together, and as I have seldom seen men work before, and a number of Portuguese fishermen, inhabitants of the island of Desertas, rendered us essential assistance, for which they received our gratitude as well as a more substantial remuneration.

At the expiration of thirty-six hours of wild excitement and unremitting toil, the transfer was effected, and the munitions of war, clothing, and stores with which the Laurel had been laden, were piled in utter confusion on the decks and in the hold of the Sea King, which was to bear that name no more.

The officers and men of both vessels were then summoned to the quarter deck of the latter, where they were informed, some of them for the first time, that she was to resign her peaceful character as well as her name, and to be transformed into a Confederate cruiser.

Captain James I. Waddell then appeared, dressed in the uniform of the Confederate States Navy, and delivered a brief but impressive address, stating that the object of the proposed cruise was to prey upon the commerce of the Government with which we were at war, thus rendering what service we could to our unfortunate country, and concluded by announcing that all who chose to join the ship in her new character, would receive fifteen pounds bounty, and be entitled to from four to seven pounds per month wages, according to their capabilities.

Captain Waddell's address was received with but little enthusiasm from the majority of those who listened to him, although, undoubtedly the greater part sympathized with our cause. But out of eighty, twenty-three only cast in their lots with the new cruiser, which then hoisted the Confederate flag, and was formally commissioned as the Confederate States' Steamer Shenandoah.

The moment of parting had come. Those who were to return in the Laurel went over the side, gave us three hearty cheers, and wished us all the success which they declined to help achieve; and we, who were to remain and follow the fortunes of the Shenandoah through weal or woe, turned to with a will, hove up our ponderous anchor from its muddy bed, and stood out to sea under steam, trusting to the God of nations and a good breeze for the safety, which, in our present situation, could only come to us from such sources.

The Shenandoah was a full rigged ship, two hundred and twenty feet in length, and thirty-five feet beam, with iron masts and lower yards. She carried royal studding sails, and was rigged with Cunningham's patent reefing topsails, and under sail with a fair breeze, with a sufficient crew to work her, we had little to apprehend from a chase. But officers and crew only numbered forty-two souls, less than half her regular complement, and consequently, for the time being, we were obliged to mainly depend upon our auxiliary engine, with which, as I have remarked in the preceding chapter, we were capable of steaming about ten knots an hour, a by no means extraordinary rate of speed for a steam cruiser.

Such were the auspices under which we commenced our adventurous cruise around the world, in a merchantman commissioned as a man-of-war, but yet to be transformed into one, whose guns lay dismounted on the deck waiting to be remounted, and have port holes cut, through which to protrude their grim muzzles, whose ammunition was piled in promiscuous heaps until a magazine could be constructed to receive it, and manned almost exclusively by officers, few, if any of whom, had ever performed a day's manual labor, who thus boldly put to sea, trusting to provide themselves with a crew from vessels yet to be captured from the enemy.

Confusion worse confounded seemed to reign on board the Shenandoah as we got under way, and short-handed as we were, it seemed a task little less than Herculean to reduce such chaos to order. But that patience and perseverance will accomplish much, is as true as trite. Every one perfectly understood that if we fell in with a United States steamer as we were then circumstanced, our race was run; and as such an abrupt terminus to our career was the reverse of desirable, every man, from the Captain downward, went resolutely to work, and ere long our combined exertions began to produce palpable results.

We left on the 20th of October, and the

3

next day we had mounted two eight-inch shell guns, and one thirty-two pounder Whitworth rifle. At the expiration of another twenty-four hours, two more eight-inch shell guns were in position, and also the mate to our Whitworth rifle. This constituted our battery with the addition of two twelve pounders aft, of which, however, we did not expect to make much use except in bringing ships to.

The carpenters also, had pierced the sides for the portholes, and things alow and aloft began to look ship-shape. Still, there was much to do in temporarily disposing of the ammunition in a place of safety, and giving the ship a general clearing up.

On the morning of the 28th, the lookout aloft reported a sail. In an instant all was excitement.

"Where away?" bawled the officer of the deck, as he hurriedly threw his glance around the horizon.

"About two points on the lee bow, sir, standing the same as we are."

"Can you make her out?"

"Aye, aye, sir, a square rigged vessel. We appear to be raising her fast. I see her better now. A barque with long mast heads, and looks like an American."

"Very good. Let me know when she shows her colors."

It would be difficult to convey an idea of the interest this brief colloquy occasioned. From every part of the ship swarmed up the little company that composed her crew, and ensconced themselves in the rigging, and wherever there was a favorable point for observation, while spy-glasses passed from hand to hand, and opinions were anxiously interchanged as to what the stranger might prove to be.

In the course of an hour we could distinguish the English ensign flying from her peak, but her appearance was so thoroughly

American that we concluded to board her and have a look at her papers.

A blank cartridge was fired across her bows, the hint was understood and she hove to, after which an officer was dispatched no board to ascertain her true character.

She proved to be the barque Monque, American built, but she had been sold to the English, as many others had been before, for fear of the Confederate cruisers. The Captain had his wife and family with him, and they seemed so cosey and contented in their little home on the sea, that I was half glad to find they were really entitled to the protection of the flag they flew, and safe from capture.

Satisfied that she was no longer an American vessel, and consequently not game for our net, we steamed off to the southward, leaving her to proceed on her voyage, which I trust was successfully accomplished.

May she never meet a worse enemy than the Shenandoah proved on that occasion!

The following morning the lookout at mast-head reported two sails in sight, one on the port beam, the other on the starboard quarter; but as yet, we were scarcely in proper condition to take the offensive where any doubt existed as to the character of our antagonists. Our number only sufficed to work two of our eight-inch guns, which would leave two thirds of our battery entirely unmanned. So, as the probabilities were that either of the strangers were far stronger numerically, we reluctantly permitted them to proceed on their way unmolested.

On the 30th, about nine o'clock in the morning, another sail was reported about three points on the port bow. It proved to be a barque, standing to the southward and westward.

We immediately got up steam, and proceeded in chase, and in about two hours, brought her to in the usual manner, by firing a blank cartridge across her bows. As she displayed the American flag from her peak, a boat was lowered, and a prize crew with two officers were sent on board to take charge of her.

On reaching the vessel, we informed the Captain that his craft was a prize to the Confederate States of America, and ordered him to get his papers and proceed on board of our ship.

He hesitated for a moment and then disappeared down the companion-way, and after a brief absence, returned to the deck with a tin box containing his documents, and in company with one of our officers, went on board the Shenandoah.

The Alina was condemned, and it fell to my lot to return with the Captain to say "good-by" to his ship, and bring away his clothing, and any other little personal property he might wish to preserve.

That he felt his misfortune keenly was

evident, although he manfully strove to conceal it under a cool, nonchalant exterior.

"I tell you what, Maty," he said, as we were returning from this, to him, sad errand, "I've a daughter at home that that craft yonder was named for, and it goes against me cursedly to see her destroyed."

"Neither myself nor my brother officers have any disposition to do you a personal injury," I answered. "Our orders are to prey upon the commerce of the United States, and in carrying them out, private individuals have to suffer, as the widows and orphans of the South have done and are doing from the invading armies acting under the instructions of your Government."

"I know it is only the fortune of war, and I must take my chances with the rest," the Captain said, resolutely, "but it's d—d hard, and I only hope I shall have an opportunity of returning your polite attentions before this muss is over, that's all."

By this time the crew of the Alina had been transferred to the Shenandoah, each old shell-back disconsolately bringing with him the bag that contained his dunnage, and were confined in single irons, and then our carpenters went off to the prize armed with augurs with which to scuttle her.

In the course of an hour they returned, having performed their duty, and I stood leaning over the quarter railing, watching, with a curious heart-heaviness that none but a sailor can understand, to see the gallant old barque sink into her ocean grave.

About four o'clock her stern suddenly settled, her bows reared high in the air, as if in indignant deprecation of such sacrilegious treatment at the hands of seamen, and with all sail set she went down right bravely.

It was the first time I ever saw a vessel sink at sea, and I confess it was some time ere I could fully recover from the unpleasant feelings the sight engendered. A sailor learns to love a ship as something almost animate; and to see one deserted in mid-ocean by those who have been her guardians, and slowly settling in the unfathomable waters, is almost like standing beside a death-bed to watch the sinking away of a soul into the ocean of eternity.

But I was fated to have a large experience in this direction ere the Shenandoah and I finally parted company.

The Alina was captured in 15° 15′ north latitude, and 26° 44′ west longitude, and was valued at ninety-five thousand dollars. Six of her crew joined us, greatly to our satisfaction, for we sadly needed such an accession to our numbers, and received the same bounty as those who shipped at the Island of Desertas. The rest were confined in the top-gallant forecastle, while the officers were accommodated in the ward room and treated with every consideration, which I need scarcely say they heartily appreciated, especially the Captain, who remarked to me that he little anticipated such kindness from an enemy; but he declined all offers of refreshment, nor could I wonder, under the circumstances, at his disinclination to join in our conviviality.

I subsequently became quite familiar with him, and passed many hours, first and last, in listening to the stories of his own experience, which he related with infinite gusto.

Several days now elapsed without bringing any especial incident to break the monotony of the voyage. The weather was glorious; the timely addition to our crew made the labor of working our gallant ship fall less heavily upon her company, and elated with the success that had thus far attended us, we dashed merrily forward on our course.

The thought often occurred to me, and I doubt not to many of my shipmates, that there was something almost terribly problematical as to the way and manner in which our cruise was destined to terminate, but that very uncertainty gave an additional zest to the wild, free life upon which we were entering, and surrounded with a fresh glamour of romance, our ship and the cause in which she sailed.

On the fifth of November we discovered a little fore-and-aft schooner standing to southward, and gave chase, under steam. Before eight o'clock we had made a prize of her, and she proved to be the Charter Oak, from Boston, bound to San Francisco with a general cargo.

The Captain had his wife, her sister, and a little boy on board with him, and there they were bound round Cape Horn, in that little schooner of less than one hundred and fifty tons burthen, — a noteworthy instance of Yankee perseverance and daring.

We were in want of a variety of articles in the furnishing way, particularly chairs, and concluded, without much hesitation, to help ourselves from the prize, so our boats were lowered and a party sent on board of her, to break out her hold and bring away whatever might be of use to us.

The boats returned, after several hours' absence, loaded to the water's edge with sofas, chairs, small tables, and an almost endless variety of preserved fruits and vegetables, among the rest a quantity of canned tomatoes, which lasted us about six months, and formed an agreeable addition to our commissariat.

Having helped ourselves to what we wished, and transferred the ladies, officers, and crew to our own ship, the schooner was set on fire, and we steamed away to the southward, a light wind blowing from the northeast, and the sea almost without a ripple.

The prisoners taken from the Charter Oak were confined in single irons and placed in the top-gallant forecastle, and accommodations were found for the officers, the ladies, and the little boy, in the ward room.

All were in fine spirits as we glided away from the scene of our last achievement. Even the Captain of our last prize I noticed walking the poop with his wife, with a very much-at-home and perfectly contented air.

For the next three days all hands were busy in putting together and setting up our new furniture, and in disposing of the other contributions which the Charter Oak had poured into our treasury. Everything in the shape of edibles was equally divided among the messes fore and aft. In all things on the Shenandoah it was share and share alike.

I should mention that as soon as it could be arranged, the after cabin on the starboard side was given up to the use of the ladies and the little boy, and it was amusing to notice with what amazement our fair prisoners received the courtesy with which we endeavored to alleviate their unpleasant position. That they had anticipated rude and perhaps brutal treatment from their captors was evident, and not unnaturally perhaps, as all sorts of sensational stories had been circulated in regard to the doings of other Confederate cruisers; and who does not know that humanity is prone to listen to and believe any recital of horror that keeps within the boundary of possibility. We were not sorry however, to have an opportunity of disabusing the minds of two Northern ladies of the notion that Confederate men-of-war's-men were a sort of revised edition of East India Sepoys.

On the 8th, about eleven A. M. a lookout on the foretop-sail yard reported a sail in sight, and as usual, everything was instantly in commotion. As there was only a light breeze blowing, we got up steam and proceeded in chase, and were not long in overhauling her. We showed the English colors, whereupon she hoisted the United States flag, which, of course, sealed her doom.

As usual, a boat was sent on board, which returned in about half an hour with the Captain and his papers, from whom we learned that our prize was the Barque D. Godfrey from Boston, bound to Valparaiso with a cargo of lumber and salt beef. Of the latter commodity we determined to lay in a supply sufficient to last us for the cruise, and a gang of carpenters and men were sent on board to break out her hold. This, however, was found to be such a laborious task that we decided to give it up and destroy her as she was.

By six o'clock her officers and crew were taken off, after which the bulkheads in the cabin and pantry were knocked down by a few blows of the carpenter's hatchet and thrown in a pile on the floor. A match was applied, and in fifteen minutes the flames were bursting through the skylights, and the work of destruction had begun.

It was an imposing scene. Darkness had settled around us when the rigging and sails took fire, but every rope could be seen as distinctly as upon a painted canvas, as the flames made their way from the deck, and writhed upward like fiery serpents. Soon the yards came thundering down by the run as the lifts and halyards yielded to the devouring element, the standing rigging parted like blazing flax, and the spars simultaneously went by the board and left the hulk wrapped from stem to stern in one fierce blaze, like a floating, fiery furnace.

While this was passing, her late commander paced the quarter-deck with folded arms and contracted brow, gazing out upon the ruin he was powerless to avert, with what feelings I could well imagine.

"That was a vessel which has done her duty well for forty years," he said to one of my brother officers, as she finally disappeared. "She has faced old Boreas in every part of the world, in the service of her master, and after such a career, to be destroyed by men on a calm night, on this tropical sea, is too bad — too bad!"

"It is but one of the results of the terrible war raging at home," remarked one of the ladies who had been a silent witness of the scene. "Would to God it was over! that the destruction of life and property by sea and land might cease."

"War is a bad thing, there's no denying it," resumed the Captain; "bad enough on land, where at least you've a solid foundation under you, but infinitely worse at sea, where it destroys the few planks that you have learned to trust to keep you from going to Davy Jones's. There is no sight so awful to a sailor as a ship on fire, even when, as in this instance, you know there is no human being on board; but there's no use in grumbling."

Our last prize was captured in latitude 4° 42′ north, and longitude 28° 24′ west, and was valued at thirty-six thousand dollars.

We had now on board about forty prisoners; ten had joined the Shenandoah, and we were anxious to dispose of the others.

An opportunity soon offered. On the following day a sail was discovered, and we proceeded in chase, under canvas. In about three hours we came up with her, and found her to be a Danish brig, bound to Rio Janeiro. An officer was dispatched on board to ascertain if the Captain would take what prisoners we had into port. He consented to take a part of them, and we immediately sent on board those we had first captured, with our best wishes for a pleasant passage and a speedy arrival at home.

The transfer occupied an hour or two, and on parting we presented the Danish Captain with a fine chronometer we had captured from one of our prizes.

He was much pleased with the gift, and assured us he should always retain it, in remembrance of the Shenandoah and the cause she represented.

On the 10th we captured in 4° 20′ north latitude, and 26° 39′ west longitude, the brig Susan, from Cardiff, bound to South America, but owned in New York, with a cargo of coal. She was valued at five thousand four hundred and thirty-six dollars. She was scuttled. Two of her men joined us; the rest were disposed of as our other prisoners had been.

We had captured four vessels within the last ten days, which, all things considered, we were disposed to regard as a fair business. We hoped, however, to do something more to make Uncle Sam remember us before going into the South Atlantic, for we were now in the track of ships bound out from

New York and other ports in the United States to San Francisco and South America.

On the 12th we captured the Kate Prince, a large clipper ship of about eleven hundred tons burthen, from Cardiff, with a neutral cargo, and ransomed her for forty thousand dollars on condition of her taking the rest of our prisoners into port. If our last prize had not had two ladies on her passenger list, I believe we should have burned her, but we had a pair of our fair enemies already in charge, and ungallant as the admission may sound, we had no desire to increase the number, through doubts of our ability to make them comfortable, I may add, in extenuation of our apparent churlishness.

By three o'clock the following morning our ship was once more free from prisoners, much to our satisfaction, and the Kate Prince proceeded on her way.

The following day, Sunday, we discovered a sail which had the appearance of a little

Yankee schooner. She was a splendid sailer, and it required several hours to overhaul her, but at length, finding escape impossible, she showed the Stars and Stripes, and the usual blank cartridge fired across her bows, brought her to. It turned out to be another Boston craft, the Lizzie M. Stacey, bound to the Sandwich Islands, round the Cape of Good Hope.

No one but a Yankee skipper would thus venture half way round the world in such a vessel, but the old sea-dog did not appear to think such a trip anything worth mentioning.

Something to this intent and purport, I remarked as the old fellow came on board our ship, and was rewarded with a contemptuous laugh.

"Shiver my timbers! if there an't the most lubberly set of sailors afloat in these latitudes that I ever fell in with," he said, adding a tough old nautical oath or two by way of emphasis. "Why day before yesterday, I run across the bows of a big English ship bound to Australia, and all hands made a rush forward when I hove in sight as though I'd been the Sea Serpent or some other almighty curiosity. They invited me to come on board but there was a stiff breeze blowing at the time, and I'd no notion of losing a good run for the sake of showing off a little before a lot of chaps who seem to think nothing less than a seventy-four is safe to cross the ocean in."

"Faix, and the ould man was right," remarked the first mate, a genuine wild Irishman, aside to one of our men; "the dirthy blackguards wouldn't have appreciated the compliment of a visit from us, and what's more, my hearty, if we'd had ten guns aboard there, you wouldn't have got us without a bit of a shindy, or if the breeze had been a bit stiffer, we'd given her the square sail, and all h—l couldn't have caught her."

There was truth in this. Had she been armed the Lizzie M. Stacey would certainly never have surrendered without a tussle, and with a favorable wind, I am inclined to believe she would have shown us a clean pair of heels. Could we have spared the necessary men to man her, we should have put one of our rifle guns on board and commissioned her as a tender to our ship, but as yet we were too short-handed for such an achievement, and she was reluctantly doomed to the same fate as her predecessors. Two of her crew joined us, and the rest were placed in the top-gallant forecastle in single irons. The officers of course received the customary courtesies which, however, were pretty much thrown away upon the Captain, who was the most unapproachable old curmudgeon I ever encountered. To get a civil word out of him was simply impossible, but the Mate took kindly to his altered fortunes, and, in a day or two, could spin a kuffer with any one on board.

Our last prize was valued at fifteen thousand dollars, and was captured in 1° 43′ north latitude, and 28° 24′ west longitude.

Our cruise in the North Atlantic was now finished. It had been brief in duration, but enough had been accomplished to give the Shenandoah such a reputation as would be apt to insure her officers and crew anything but a cordial reception from one of Uncle Sam's cruisers, should we have the luck to fall in with one.

CHAPTER III.

FROM THE "LINE" TO ST. PAUL'S ISLAND.

ON the 15th of November we crossed the line, and the usual ceremonies attendant upon that event on board a man-of-war were not neglected.

It is a custom as old as sailing, for aught I know, for every armed vessel on passing the equator to receive a visit from his aquatic Godship Neptune, who is supposed to hold his court in that locality, suffering no ship to pass until he has satisfied himself by personal inspection that there are none on board but regularly initiated sailors; that is, those who have previously crossed the line and submitted to his initiatory rites. We had a number of novices among officers and men, and consequently the event was anticipated with even more than ordinary interest.

It was just gone eight bells in the evening when a rough voice over the bows was heard hailing the ship.

"What's wanting?" said the officer of the deck.

"Heave to. I want to come on board," was the surly response.

The requisite orders were given, and a few moments after a gigantic figure was seen ascending the side, dressed in an oil-skin coat, and wearing a wig of Manilla yarn, which, at a little distance, had the appearance of yellowish curly hair.

He was accompanied by another grotesque figure representing his wife, and the two were followed by a third, who was supposed to be His Majesty's confidential barber, provided with the utensils of his calling, which consisted of a bucket of slush, and a preposterous razor, about three feet long, manufactured from an iron hoop. His Godship carried an immense speaking-trumpet under his arm, a trident in his right hand, and stepped upon the deck with all the dignity his assumed position warranted.

"What ship is this?" he said, in an authoritative voice.

"The Confederate cruiser Shenandoah," replied the officer of the deck, touching his hat.

"Are there any of my subjects on board who have never crossed the line before?" was the next question.

"There are several, I believe."

"Bring them before me!" continued his Godship, and thereupon such of the company as had already passed the ordeal dispersed in search of the novices.

We found them stowed away in every imaginable place of concealment, but they were scented out, and dragged before the Ocean Deity, where they were solemnly lathered from the slush-bucket, and shaved with the iron hoop, according to immemorial usage.

The frolic was kept up until a late hour, and an additional zest was added to the festivities by the fact that two or three of our youngsters actually believed that they had been in the presence of the veritable Neptune, and it was only after the expiration of a considerable time that they discovered that they had been imposed upon by some of their own shipmates.

We were now steering to the southward, in the hope of falling in with vessels bound from San Francisco to New York, round Cape Horn.

We had struck the southeast trade winds, which wafted us along at the rate of nine or ten knots an hour, with all sail set. The weather was delightful, and in high spirits we sped merrily on our way.

Some days had now elapsed without bringing us in sight of any sail we might lawfully capture, but the time could scarcely be said to hang heavily upon our hands. We had an excellent library on board comprising over six hundred volumes, and with reading, social games, and story telling, we managed to pass the period of inactivity quite felicitously.

Of course our lookouts were constantly on the alert for Yankee craft which are readily recognized by the peculiarity of their rig; but although ships of every other nationality were flitting around us from time to time, those we sought failed to cross our path. Occasionally we exchanged signals and reckoning with those we met by the way, but for the most part we avoided social intercourse.

The 26th found us in 27° 30′ south latitude, an excellent run from the line.

About six o'clock that afternoon we gave chase to a vessel which however proved to be English, much to the annoyance of every one, as we were beginning to feel impatient for another dash at the enemy, and our prisoners, especially Captain Archer of the Lizzie M. Stacey, were anxiously hoping that the next prize would be ransomed upon condition of taking them into port.

On the 28th we sighted several sails, but our Captain, for some reason best known to himself, did not give chase to any of them.

On the 4th of December we discovered a craft which had the general appearance of an American, and we stood in chase and overhauled her, the United States flag flying at our peak. She flew the Italian colors, but looked so thoroughly Yankee that we sent a couple of officers, dressed in blue uniform, to keep up our assumed character on board, to have a look at her papers.

It turned out as we feared. She was American built, but had been sold to the Italians to keep her out of the hands of enterprising gentlemen in our line of business.

About four o'clock the same afternoon, another sail was reported, which for a time puzzled us all, until one of our old sea-dogs pronounced her to be an American whaler, which eventually proved to be the case.

As we steamed near her she hoisted the American flag, whereupon we stopped our engines and sent a boat with a prize crew on board, and in a little time, her Captain, having his papers in charge, was with us.

She was a bluff-bowed, square-sterned, old-fashioned craft, from New Bedford, of about four hundred tons, and had been whaling for nearly fifty years. She had been out about four months, and had taken but one whale, which she was engaged in "cutting in" when we captured her.

Her commander, Captain Worth, was one of the finest specimens of an American sailor I have ever met. Brave, generous, and open-hearted, he was one of those men who inspire an enemy with respect and a feeling of regret that the stern necessity of war involves their capture. He had been a shipmaster twenty-five years, and of course could not avoid feeling deeply the destruction of his old craft in which he had faced so many perils, and earned an honorable fame in his calling. But nothing of this appeared in his face as he came over the side and saluted us with a courteous "Good afternoon, gentlemen. You have a fine ship here for a cruiser."

"Yes, sir," responded the officer of the deck, "and that vessel of yours looks as if she was familiar with travelling salt water."

"Yes, she was laid on the stocks before you and I were thought of," he answered, leaning nonchalantly against the bulwarks, and thereupon fell into an easy and affable conversation with the officer of the deck, upon whales and whaling, as naturally as though we were a brother whaler, and he had come on board of us for a "gam."

Ere he left us, he had won the respect and esteem of every man on board the Shenandoah.

It is generally the case that whalers are better provisioned than any other class of vessels; consequently we considered the present opportunity a good one to replenish our own stores, and therefore lay alongside our prize till morning, her crew in the mean time being placed in irons, — a precautionary measure we disliked to adopt, but our own safety required it.

As soon as it was light, the whaler's crew were released, and assisted, with the best grace they could, in transferring their own supplies, consisting principally of flour and bread, to the Shenandoah. This occupied several hours, and during the time a number of our officers went off to see what a whaler was like, and inspect the blubber which had been cut from the sea-monster which was still moored alongside.

Late in the afternoon, having secured what we desired from the Barque Edward, we set her on fire, and got under way, taking three of her boats in tow and steering for the Island of Tristan d'Acunha, where our Captain had resolved to land what prisoners he had on board.

Early the following morning the island was in sight looming up some eight thousand three hundred feet above the level of the sea, and by eight o'clock we had it on our port beam. Steaming slowly round to discover a suitable place for landing, we at last saw the English flag flying from a flag-staff on shore, and hove to, and the boats we had been towing were hauled alongside, and the prisoners with their clothes and bedding placed in them.

While this was going on, we observed a boat coming off from the shore, and ere long she was rocking under our quarter, and its principal occupant was offering for sale milk, eggs, chickens, and fresh meat, commodities I need hardly say for which we were quite ready to barter.

It was the first time the Islanders had seen the flag that floated from our peak, and to what nationality it belonged they could not imagine, nor was their astonishment in any wise diminished when we informed them that our ship was a Confederate cruiser, and we had thirty-five prisoners which we proposed contributing to their population.

"And where the devil did you get your prisoners?" queried one of the mystified natives.

"From a whaler not far from here," responded one of our officers.

"Just so, to be sure; and what became of the whaler?"

"We burned her up."

"Whew! Is that the way you dispose of what vessels you fall in with?"

"If they belong to the United States; not otherwise."

"Well, my hearty, you know your own business, but my notion is that these sort of pranks will get you into the devil's own muss before you are through with it. What your quarrel with the United States is I don't know, but I swear I don't believe they'll stand this kind of work."

The astonishment our proceedings occasioned the residents of Tristan d'Acunha (there are only about forty of them all told), and their evident conviction that our calling was not likely to be a very safe one, did not stand in the way of their commercial proclivities, and we soon struck up a bargain for a quantity of fresh beef, which, however, had to be killed before it could be delivered; but the time was disposed of by getting the prisoners safely off, and seeing that they were provided with coffee, tea, sugar, and all other articles necessary for their temporal sojourn.

At last the Islanders came off with the provisions we had purchased, and received in exchange flour and pilot bread. We also procured of them a couple of sheep, and after making these additions to our commissariat, we steamed away, leaving the island on our starboard quarter.

This last prize furnished us with a new phase of cruising experience. Heretofore our prisoners had been transferred to some prize selected for the purpose, and sent on their way, if not rejoicing, at least reasonably well satisfied with such a method of egress from one of the unpleasant predicaments of war; but now for the first time we had left our captured foes on an island of the South Atlantic, thousands of miles from their homes, where they might have to remain for many weary months, ere a passing ship would take them off (though it was of course possible they might be relieved in a week), and none of us were quite satisfied with the part we were necessitated to play, but I question whether our Yankee acquaintances stood much in need of our sympathy after all. They had the free range of a charming island, where reigned perennial summer; besides, there were a number of the gentler sex in want of mates, I learned, and where there are pretty women so circumstanced, there can sailors be happy.

I may mention, *en passant*, that they have rather a primitive way of celebrating the nuptial contract on Tristan d'Acunha. The oldest inhabitant, one of the ubiquitous sons of Connecticut, of course, who stranded there some five and twenty years ago, and drives a thriving trade in beef and poultry with the whalers that put in there, has assumed to himself the prerogative of uniting in the holy bonds of wedlock the matrimonially disposed, and he performs the service, I understood, as much to the satisfaction of the parties interested as it could be done by surpliced priest before the chancel rails.

On the following day we discovered that our engine was injured, one of the propeller bands being broken in two places, and it was at first rumored that we would have to put into some port for repairs; but after a thorough investigation it was decided to endeavor to temporarily remedy the difficulty where we were, and in the meantime to depend upon our canvas.

I ought to have mentioned that before capturing the barque Edward, we overhauled a sail, the Adelaide, from Baltimore, and she was about being consigned to the fate of her predecessors that had fallen into our hands, when we discovered that she belonged to a Mr. Pendergrass, a Baltimorean and a Southern sympathizer, which saved her from sacrifice, but the discovery was only made after her bulkheads had been demolished and a good deal of miscellaneous damage done preparatory to burning. The cargo, however, not being the property of any of our friends, was ransomed for forty thousand dollars.

On the 14th we were scudding along under topsails, at the rate of ten or eleven knots an hour, with a high sea running, which increased tremendously as we neared the Cape of Good Hope. To any one but a sailor it would hardly have seemed possible that a vessel could live in such a sea as we encountered in this locality. It ran absolutely mountains high, and had not the Shenandoah been an excellent sea-boat, among her other admirable characteristics, we should have felt considerable apprehension, although instances are comparatively rare of vessels foundering from sheer stress of weather. Numerous birds were following in our wake, and among them were the albatross, cape pigeon, and stormy petrel, or, as the latter are better known among seamen, Mother Carey's chickens.

On the 15th, our reckoning showed us to be about five hundred and fifty miles to the southward and westward of the Cape and the ocean still pursuing its mad antics with unabated fury, but over it our gallant vessel scud, as easily as the birds skimmed the air astern.

Our position, however, was becoming anything but comfortable. To get a meal in Christian fashion was the next thing to impossible. The steward, after much devious navigating would succeed at last in placing it upon the table, and the next moment a heavy lurch of the ship would scatter dishes and contents in every direction. Once, not satisfied with such a piece of impertinence, old Neptune sent a sea over our starboard quarter, which came pouring down upon us like a cataract, and the remnant of our dinner previously disposed around the cabin floor by the first accident, was by the second, submerged under a couple of feet of water.

During the prevalence of a heavy and continuous gale like the present, a man-of-war presents a curious scene. The battery is secured with extra tackles, preventer-braces and backstays are rove and taughtened, hatches battened down, and men are stationed at the relieving tackles in case the wheel ropes part, to prevent the ship from broaching to.

These precautionary measures taken, or perhaps the ship is hove to under close-reefed topsails, fore storm staysail, main trysail, and a tarpaulin in the mizzen rigging, little parties of men may be seen congregated on different parts of the berth deck, each listening to some tough yarn, spun by some old shell back of their number.

Suddenly the sound of the boatswain's call is heard, sharp and shrill above the howling of the tempest, and for the moment conversation ceases, and every man anxiously awaits to learn the nature of the summons. It is nothing any more serious this time than to call all hands to the agreeable duty of "splicing the main brace," and in an instant there is a general rush for the deck, where the grog is served to each in turn.

To a landsman it may seem the height of recklessness to serve out any intoxicating beverage at such a time, to a ship's company, but the omission of such an item in the routine of their lives would probably engender a general feeling of dissatisfaction more to be dreaded than any trifling excess in which they would be likely to indulge.

On that day the storm culminated. It was sublime beyond description, and we drove before it, at the rate of eleven knots an hour, under close reefed topsails and reefed foresail, About five o'clock that afternoon, we took a sea about amidships, which poured down the main hatch, to the summary discomfiture of a knot of the boys who were enjoying themselves by listening to a "twister" of more than ordinary interest.

Such were some of the specimens of "life on the ocean wave," that we encountered while working up toward the Cape of Good Hope, a name suggestive of good omens, but our experience did not tend to confirm the reputation that has gone abroad concerning the peaceful proclivities of the elements thereabouts.

On the 16th, it was still blowing a gale from the northward and westward, and we were running before it at the rate of eleven or twelve knots an hour under a light spread of canvas. About eight o'clock in the evening a tremendous sea came over our quarter, carrying away everything movable in its track, and thoroughly drenching about half our officers and crew. The ship now seemed to be flooded fore and aft, the greater part of the time, but such good precautionary measures had been taken that comparatively little water found its way below.

At twelve o'clock the next day, a wave of mountain dimensions came surging down upon us, and rearing its mighty crest, like a very demon of the ocean intent upon our destruction, discharged a cataract of water, whose weight could only have been estimated by hundreds of tons, upon our devoted deck. It was a moment of fearful anxiety. Fore and aft the water stood level with the top of the bulwarks, — the ship lost her headway and trembled as did Goliah when the pebble from the shepherd boy's sling penetrated his brazen head-gear, and like Goliah she would in a few brief moments have sunk to rise no more, had not our dauntless crew in obedience to an order from the officer of the deck, uttered as coolly as though it was the most ordinary occasion instead of a matter of life and death, sprung forward with axes, and dashed out the ports, thus affording egress to the mass of water which was pressing us down, like the hand of doom, into the treacherous bosom of the Atlantic.

That day the gale finally blew itself out, but our troubles were as yet by no means over, for as the wind went down, the sea increased, if that was possible, and for three or four succeeding days, the Shenandoah was buffeted, tossed, and knocked about, as an empty bottle might be driven in the wake of a steamship, but we managed to hold on our course toward Australia.

It had been my fortune to spend four Christmas days at sea, far removed from all the festivities and merry-making that characterizes its advent upon shore, but my Christmas in the Shenandoah, off the Cape of Good Hope, was the most miserable travesty of the festival I ever celebrated. We were boxing about, as I have described, at the mercy of old Neptune's irate temper, drenched with water the greater part of the time, and generally and profoundly miserable, when the anniversary of the day that brought "peace on earth, good will to men," dawned upon us. My thoughts would revert to home, to the family gathering at the Christmas dinner, to the old church with its evergreen decorations, and to the evening spent in fun and frolic.

Such was the home picture, and a more complete reverse of it could hardly be imagined, than was presented by our ship and company. In the place of pendant evergreens my eyes rested upon the smoky, swaying lamps, still dimly burning in the ward room, and instead of receiving the time-honored salutations from family friends, and bright-faced girls, whose lips give so sweet an intonation to the old phrase, I heard it from rough-bearded men, sunburned and swarthy, and in place of preparing for a gay holiday, I donned my sou'wester and moodily made my way to the deck to stand a four hours' watch.

Our cook, good, conscientious man that he was, put all his science in requisition, and strained his resources to the utmost, to achieve a good dinner, but the old goose upon which he tried his skill, was, I verily believe, the identical fowl that Commodore Noah took with him on his first and last cruise. All that fire could do to render digestible that tough old specimen, was done, and in due time we grimly devoured him, but not before he had been several times rescued from his native element beneath the table, where he had been tossed by the heaving of the ship.

My solemn advice to the world at large is, never to go off the Cape of Good Hope in a cruiser to enjoy Christmas.

On the 29th our eyes were greeted once more by the welcome sight of a ship. As it was astern, we shortened sail and waited for her to come up with us.

By three o'clock she was near enough to

"read bunting," and by way of testing her nationality, we showed the English flag. Up went the Stars and Stripes to the peak of the stranger, a welcome sight to us, whereupon we lowered our borrowed ensign, and, much to the consternation, I have no doubt, of our new acquaintance, ran up the flag of the Confederacy, and fired a blank cartridge across her bows. She immediately hove to, and we sent a boat to bring off the Captain and his papers. The Captain of the stranger soon reached us, and reported his craft to be the barque Delphine, of Bangor, Maine, seventy days out from London, in ballast, and bound for Akyab, Arabia, for a cargo of rice. The Captain informed us that his wife and child were on board, and also that his steward was encumbered with a helpmate. The Captain's wife was ill, and with such a sea running, he feared it would be dangerous to attempt to bring her off.

Captain Waddell expressed his regret at

the inconvenience to which he was compelled to subject the ladies, but assured him that no danger should befall them, as our life-boat with six good oarsmen, should be detailed for the service.

To object was of course useless, so with as good a grace as possible our prisoners set out in the life-boat on their unpleasant expedition.

In due time the life-boat returned with the two women and little boy, the Captain of the prize and such articles of personal property as he desired to retain. The Captain's wife woman like, brought with her a canary bird in its cage, and if a bandbox containing her best bonnet had been added to her baggage, it would have been complete.

Soon after two or three other boats put off from the barque containing her crew, who were at once confined in single irons, and placed in the top-gallant forecastle.

One of our officers with two or three men

had remained on board the Delphine to fire her as soon as her own company had been safely removed; and we, of the Shenandoah, were now anxiously pacing the decks, watching for the first indications that this duty had been performed. Night closed around us before the first forked tongue of fire, issuing from the companion-way of the fated barque, warned us that the destroying element had commenced its work. Rapidly the flames gathered headway, casting a fierce, lurid glow over the heaving bosom of the ocean; from doors, windows, and hatchways they burst forth like the vengeful spirit of destruction, wound up the spars, stretched out upon the yards, swiftly enveloping shrouds, sails, and halyards in one splendid, fiery ruin; and standing out, strongly revealed against the darkening sky, the burning vessel surged and tossed, a holocaust to the God of War.

But while all this was passing, the lookouts were closely scanning the watery expanse that intervened between us and the burning ship, to discover our boat returning. The darkness of the night and the heavy sea that was running, rendered us unpleasantly apprehensive that she might have swamped on her passage back, and as a precautionary measure, lanterns were run up in the rigging to advise them of our whereabouts. At last we saw them, just rising on the summit of a mighty wave, less than a hundred yards to windward, and presently after we distinguished the rough voice of the officer in command hailing us.

"Ahoy, there!" he said; "throw us a line!"

The request was complied with, — a coil of rope sailed away from the deck of the Shenandoah through the air, rendered half opaque by the spray of breaking waves; it was caught by our comrades, — in another moment they were alongside, and presently after we had them safe on board, and were once more standing on our course.

The after-cabin on the starboard side was appropriated to the Captain of our last prize and his wife, and in every respect they were treated far more like passengers than prisoners, but never was courtesy more completely thrown away upon an enemy. They not only utterly failed to appreciate, in any degree, the manner in which they were treated while they were with us, but indulged in the most scandalous romance at our expense after they got on shore. This was all well enough no doubt, but if our friend of the Delphine had fallen into our hands a second time, we, knowing the reputation he had given us, would have taught him by experience ere we parted company, something of the dark side of the picture which a prisoner of war has occasion to inspect.

For an hour or more the Captain of the Delphine paced up and down the deck, accompanied by his wife, watching his blazing vessel, now rapidly dropping below the horizon. I could not help pitying him. He was a third owner, and probably had there invested the savings of half a lifetime of patient toil. To see the fruits of so many years swept away in an hour, might well try the philosophy of the best of men.

The 30th of December found us still standing toward Australia, with all sail set on a bowline. It was one of the most beautiful days we had seen since leaving England. The air was soft and balmy, like the month of May in our own sunny South, and the heavy sea we had encountered for so many days seemed to have exhausted its mad passion, and had died away into the long undulating swell almost invariably encountered off soundings.

During my watch that morning, I had a long conversation with the Captain of our last prize, in the course of which he informed me that he was a good deal chagrined when he first came on board of us and discovered to what an incipient man-of-war he had surrendered, without an effort at escape. He had expected, when he came off to us, to find a cruiser with all her guns in working order, and men to work them, — a craft, in fact, that in five minutes' time would be ready to blow him out of water, but "distance lent enchantment to the view," he discovered, when he saw our real condition, and he bitterly lamented that he had not at least made the attempt to show us his heels.

I very much incline to the opinion that had he shaken out his canvas, going at the rate he was, he would have given us the slip before, short-handed as we were, we could have made sail, or brought our guns to bear.

The new year, wearing all the languid beauty of a Southern clime, opened upon me just as I was about to be relieved from duty on deck. The weather was fine, with a light, variable wind blowing, and the stars threw their silvery shimmer over the quiet water. Every one on board, save the officer of the deck, the quartermaster, the lookout, and the man at the wheel, were wrapped in slumber. Such were my surroundings when the ship's bell, striking the hour of twelve, announced the death of eighteen hundred sixty-four and the birth of eighteen hundred sixty-five.

Many thousand miles from home and friends, with the broad Atlantic all around us, and our adventurous career just begun, we did not forget the day, and at eight o'clock in the morning we unfurled our banner to the breeze, and there at our peak it waved, the emblem of a young nation which for four years had struggled, God only knows with what self-denying patience and resolution, for liberty.

The next day we sighted the Island of St. Paul, in the Indian Ocean, and stood in with a view of regulating our chronometer. By one o'clock we had approached as near its southern extremity as we desired to venture, and let go our anchor.

CHAPTER IV.

FROM ST. PAUL'S TO MELBOURNE, AUSTRALIA.

ST. PAUL'S ISLAND is situated several hundred miles to the eastward of the Cape of Good Hope, and is comparatively seldom visited. To sight land is always agreeable after a three months' cruise, and there were many applicants for permission to go on shore, this being the first opportunity that had offered since we set sail from Madeira, and excepting the Island of Tristan d'Acunha, was the first land we had seen.

Leave was extended to a number of the officers, and they presently pulled off in one of the quarter boats, well provided with all the requisite paraphernalia for fishing, having in contemplation a raid upon the finny denizens of the ocean, which seemed to have a peculiar *penchant* for congregating near these shores. There was many a longing glance cast after the receding boat by the weary voyagers, who had been so long confined within the walls of our floating fortress, and more than one discontented face might have been seen moving up and down the deck until the little craft, with its more fortunate occupants, rounded a point of land which jutting far out into the sea, formed a partially landlocked bay and disappeared.

Ere long the lookout at mast-head reported land to the northward, and an inspection of the chart showed it to be the Island of Amsterdam, distant from St. Paul's about forty miles. The Island of St. Dennis makes up the group, and is the residence of the Governor whose official sway extends over the three.

Governor Rondoney was formerly an officer in the French army, and is a gentleman of considerable ability and personal popularity. He is said to keep up a fine establishment and to wear his honors right bravely.

The climate of these islands is delightful, and with a fine soil, and all the auxiliaries peculiar to a semi-tropical country, I was somewhat surprised to learn that they were but sparsely inhabited. Their out-of-the-way location has no doubt something to do with it, as that circumstance would naturally deter foreigners from settling there to any great extent. They carry on a desultory trade with Madagascar, and some ports on the mainland of the eastern coast of Africa, but this comprises all their commerce, and nearly all of the few vessels that touch there have no more important business than the regulation of their chronometers, an important item with the vessels to be sure, but not a very productive source of revenue to Governor Rondoney's dominions.

A little before six o'clock the boat returned, literally loaded down with fish of excellent quality, and the excursionists were accordingly in the best of spirits. They paid dearly for their amusement, however. All of them were fearfully sunburned by the strong reflection from the water, and there was not a pair of hands that had not been thoroughly blistered by their long pull at the oars. They had hoped to capture a seal or two, as these animals are frequently found in the vicinity, but failing in this, they turned covetous eyes upon a penguin which they found in the possession of three old French shellbacks, left there some time before by a wandering ship, with whom they struck up an acquaintance and brought his aquatic fowl-ship off in triumph.

These three French worthies had things very much their own way on St. Paul's, they being in fact the only residents. They were engaged in catching and salting fish, with which to freight a vessel then absent on a voyage to Madagascar, where a ready market was found for that kind of provender.

Before we sailed, they came off to pay us a visit, and brought with them a quantity of chickens, which they exchanged with us for pocket handkerchiefs, an article of which they certainly stood in need, as indeed they did of various other etceteras of civilized life, but upon the whole, the old fellows seemed to be rather enjoying themselves in this Robinson Crusoish way.

The other two islands are not quite so badly off by way of inhabitants, and the one which has the honor to be the residence of His Excellency the Governor, boasts of a considerable village; but if the labor of ruling bears any proportion to the number of the ruled, I incline to the opinion that Governor Rondoney's official duties are not arduous.

I should have mentioned before that when we first sighted St. Paul's, the Captain of our last prize took the conceit into his crotchety head that we contemplated no less a practical joke than leaving himself and his company there with the agreeable prospect of remaining perhaps for years, subsisting as best they could, ere an opportunity would offer of a return to the world,

I observed his wife anxiously scanning the beautiful solitude as we were standing in, and the tears with which her eyes were heavy furnished me with a ready clue to the apprehension under which she was suffering.

"Did you suppose, Madam," I said, by way of setting her fears at rest, "that you were to be left in this out-of-the-way spot?"

"That was my husband's expectation," she answered, "and I presumed of course that his fears were not without foundation."

"Let me assure you to the contrary then, and be good enough to inform me how your husband or yourself came to imagine that the commander of the Shenandoah was capable of leaving a whole ship's company in such a place."

She hesitated for a moment, and then, with a furtive glance at my face, said:

"Why, they tell terrible stories at home about the outrages committed upon defenceless men and women by your rebel cruisers. The papers have been full of them, and I naturally supposed they were founded on fact, at least."

I could not restrain a smile at the naiveté with which our lady prisoner admitted the entertainment of a pretty well-defined conviction that she was in the hands of veritable pirates, who were only restrained from flying the black flag, with its pleasingly suggestive skull and cross-bones, because, for the time being, it suited their convenience to sail under another, little if any more reputable in her estimation; but I suppressed any stronger demonstrations of merriment, and upon my expressing a desire to see some of the literature to which she referred, she brought from her state-room a file of an illustrated New York publication, wherein was a marvellous narrative, written by a lady with a multitude of initials. I subsequently read it through, greatly amused, I must confess, at its stupendous absurdities. In the course of the story the Confederate cruiser Alabama was introduced, and her officers and crew represented as a pack of rascals, whom Morgan the buccaneer, or the leader of the Indian Sepoys would have expelled from their several commands, lest they should become contaminated by evil associations.

The grotesque blunders by the authoress when she undertook to mount the nautical horse, furnished a theme of amusement for the wardroom for many a day.

Having corrected our chronometers, which, however, were only found to be a few seconds out of the way, we were about setting sail when we observed a ship coming round the Island, and hauled up to intercept her. It had been some time since a plump fish had come to our net, and all earnestly hoped the stranger might have the honor of belonging to the universal Yankee nation.

As she neared us we showed the English flag to which she responded by displaying the flag of the Netherlands; and as a closer inspection made her out thoroughly un-American in appearance, we allowed her to proceed on her voyage unmolested.

The next day, January 3rd, we set studding sails for the first time, but were too short handed to do it in scientific, man-of-war style. We cherished the hope that the fine weather that had at last overtaken us was to continue, but the hope proved delusive, and the next morning found us under single reefed top-sails, a wet deck fore and aft, and hatches battened down to keep the water from the berth deck.

On the 5th the wind moderated, and we

once more cracked on all sail, anxious to reach Australia as soon as possible. The prisoners had naturally begun to tire of their unaccustomed inactivity, and to pine for the moment when they would be once more free, although they were made, in every respect, as comfortable as circumstances permitted.

The Captain and his wife had the privilege of walking the poop deck whenever they chose, and availed themselves of the permission very freely; but the old fellow made himself so continually and unmitigatedly disagreeable that our officers perforce avoided him, and as heartily wished to be rid of him and his ship's company as they were to discontinue our acquaintance.

That afternoon we overhauled the ship Nimrod, of American build, but transferred to British owners out of compliment to the Confederate Navy, a mark of respect which we reciprocated by not taking the liberty of changing her place of destination.

Her captain, however, a grand-looking old fellow, with tremendous white whiskers, which gave him something of the general look of a venerable polar bear, came off in his gig, to return the call of our boarding officer, and brought with him a dozen of fine old Otard as a present to Captain Waddell.

The compliment was fully appreciated, and a scene of festivity followed on board the Shenandoah that I shall not soon forget. It was but a brief sojourn that the Captain of the Nimrod made with us, but for weeks afterwards his name was often coupled by our officers with enthusiastic praise, and I only trust he has as pleasant reminiscences of his visit to the rebel cruiser.

For some time afterwards nothing of special interest occurred. It was the same monotonous story of uneventful ocean life. The lookouts regularly mounted to their perches and swept the horizon with watchful eyes for wayfarers, that we might lawfully bid to proceed no farther, but none such crossed our path.

At last our reckoning showed us to be within a day or two's sail of Australia, that mighty island continent of the Indian seas. Whereupon we got our engine into operation and steamed for port.

On the 25th, ninety days out from Madeira, we sighted land, and a few hours later we passed through Port Philip Heads, the entrance to Hobson's Bay. Here the pilot boarded us, and very much astonished was that functionary when he learned the name and character of the vessel he had in charge, which it seemed had been reported as the Ship Royal Standard, fifty odd days out from London, but this erroneous impression was soon corrected by a telegraph, and we steamed on up the Bay at the rate of nine knots an hour passing a multitude of yachts, and pleasure boats of various descriptions, filled with an eager multitude, all apparently delighted to see such a ship with the Confederate flag flying, and about six o'clock we dropped our anchor off Sandridge, a small town about two miles from Melbourne.

CHAPTER V.

OUR TARRY AT MELBOURNE.

AS soon as it became generally known in Melbourne that a Confederate cruiser had arrived in the offing, a scene of excitement was inaugurated which baffles all adequate description. Crowds of people were rushing hither and thither, seeking authentic information concerning the stranger, and ere we had been an hour at anchor, a perfect fleet of boats was pulling toward us from every direction.

As yet, however, no one was permitted to board us. It was still somewhat problematical what sort of a reception was in store for us from the authorities, and that was a question that had to be answered definitely, ere we permitted our decks to be encumbered by a crowd of possible enemies under the guise of curious friends.

There was but one solitary deviation from this prohibitory rule respecting visitors. On one of the many little sail-boats rocking alongside, was an old man, whose anxiety to set foot on our decks would have been painful had it not been ludicrous. Finding a deaf ear turned to all his entreaties, as a last resort, he climbed the spar of his little vessel and watching his opportunity sprang into the mizzen chains and scrambled on board. There was something so laughably audacious in being boarded whether we would or not, by a single individual, that the officer of the deck stood gazing at the intruder apparently somewhat at a loss whether it was his duty to surrender the ship, or throw him overboard. The old fellow took advantage of this momentary hesitation to explain that he was the only genuine Confederate in the country, which circumstance he insisted, entitled him to a reception on any vessel that flew his country's flag. His logic was not firstrate, but his coolness and audacity were admirable; and these prevailing in his favor, he was allowed to remain, to his exceeding great satisfaction.

As soon as practicable, an officer was dispatched on shore to confer with the authorities, and obtain permission for our ship to remain and procure some necessary repairs. He returned before midnight, having succeeded in his mission, and the next day the Shenandoah was thrown open to the inspection of visitors.

As soon as this was known, and the news seemed to spread like wildfire, steamers and sail-boats came flocking off towards us, and all day long, and until far into the evening, were plying between our ship and the shore, bringing on board and taking away thousands of persons, all eager to say that they had visited the famous "rebel pirate."

The multitude of absurd questions with which we were plied by the gaping crowd, would have made a stoic laugh. A large percentage of our visitors seemed to entertain the notion that the human beings were removed from the vessels we captured, or not, as convenience dictated, prior to their destruction, and solemnly queried of us as to the manner in which the Yankees bore themselves while watching the approach of the devouring element upon a burning ship, or waiting to be engulfed with a scuttled one. But notwithstanding this hard character they were ready to ascribe to us, they vied with each other in showing us every courtesy in their power, and the ladies in particular were well pleased when they could secure the attendance of a grey uniform to escort them on their tour of inspection. Of a truth there are some curious phases in human nature.

The following day we were the recipients of some more tangible proof of the goodwill with which the residents of Melbourne regarded us. Each of our officers received a railroad pass to go and return from Sandridge to Melbourne on the Hobson Bay Railroad, so long as we remained in port. Invitations to dinners and balls poured in from all sides, and every one was particular to mention that he felt the warmest sympathy for the Confederate cause.

All this was agreeable enough if one did not care to examine too closely into the sincerity of these friendly demonstrations, and after ninety days at sea, it was pleasant to see the gay groups of women upon our decks, but the Shenandoah had come there to refit, not to be exhibited as a curiosity, and this continual crush and whirl of visitors put an effectual check to the real business in hand; consequently, when the first excitement had in a measure subsided, we were obliged to close our doors, and hang out a most inhospitable and peremptory "not at home" to all callers. This prohibition caused considerable heart-burnings, but necessity knows no law, and upon the whole, our popularity did not suffer. Whenever and wherever an officer appeared on shore, he was forthwith surrounded by a little conclave of sympathetic admirers, and had we accepted a tithe of the invitations we received to indulge in spirituous comforts, we should all of us, from the Captain down to the toughest old shellback in the forecastle, have been shockingly inebriated during the whole period of our sojourn.

But, after all, that tarry in Melbourne was one of the bright reminiscences of our adventurous cruise round the world. I do not suppose so much hospitality ever was or ever will be shown to another ship in that port, and there were few if any who sailed in the Shenandoah, who will not carry to their graves many pleasant memories of the days they spent on the shores of Australia.

It must not be supposed, however, that the entire population favored us, either secretly or openly. There was a strong party who firmly adhered to the cause of the United States, and these looked upon us as contumacious rebels, seeking to overthrow, by the most unjustifiable and atrocious means, a generous and beneficent government; and could they have retaliated upon us some of the depredations we had committed upon their merchant marine, our gallant ship would certainly have proceeded no further.

Ere many days we received from a friendly source, a hint that a plot was on foot to destroy the Shenandoah by means of torpedoes, and from that time forward three officers were constantly on watch at the same time, to prevent any suspicious looking boat or object from approaching. In the night time, if a boat was discovered in our vicinity, she was hailed three times, and then if a satisfactory answer was not received, our orders were peremptory to fire into her; but we were fortunately never driven to this extremity. Scarcely a night passed that there were not craft of more than doubtful character flitting around us; but at the first hail they either pulled off or rendered such an account of themselves as we were content to accept.

Hundreds of men made application to join us here, but as we had no right to ship any in a neutral port, all were denied, reluctantly, as will be readily imagined when it is remembered how much we desired to augment our numbers.

One day, I remember, an old lady came aboard with her little son. She was a Southern woman, she said, and her boy had been born in the Sunny South, and she desired Captain Waddell to take him as the only contribution she had to offer to her country, and educate him for the service. It was hard to deny such a request made in such a way, but it had to be done, and the woman with her little rebel went her way, sorrowful and disappointed.

On the 28th quite an accident occurred. A party consisting of a lady and two gentlemen were coming off in a sail-boat to visit us. The wind was blowing strong, and just as they had rounded our stern the boat capsized. Another boat chanced to be in the immediate vicinity, and fortunately all were rescued, having sustained no more serious damage than a thorough drenching in salt water, and a very considerable fright. The gentlemen, notwithstanding their saturated garments, came on board, but the lady would not make the venture in her drooping crinoline, and returned to the shore, in a decided pet at the accident which had prevented her from inspecting the cruiser.

The next day was Sunday, the grand gala-day of the week in Melbourne. We anticipated a crowded ship fore and aft, and were not disappointed. The crowd commenced coming about nine o'clock in the morning, and continued to pour in and out in an endless stream until five in the afternoon. More than seven thousand people passed over the railroad from Melbourne to Sandridge, en route for the Shenandoah, that day, besides hundreds of others who came by other modes of conveyance.

Our ship was simply *packed* with men and women from top to bottom the live-long day, and many were prevented by the pressure, from getting on board. Indeed, so great was the curiosity we excited, that had we been content to stay for six months in Melbourne, and charged an admission fee of one dollar to visitors, I believe we could have paid a large instalment upon the Confederate debt.

It had been determined to make that day the last of our receptions, as it was imperative to proceed with our refitting. A gang of caulkers were procured and went to work upon our decks with pitch and oakum, and preparations were hurried forward to remove from the ship her stores and such ponderous furniture as could be readily gotten out to lessen her draft preparatory to placing her upon the slip, where her propeller could be inspected.

A couple of lighters were hauled alongside, and into them were hoisted such articles as we desired to be rid of for the present, and this accomplished we proceeded to the slip, where we remained for ten days, though the work was expedited as rapidly as possible, alternate gangs of men working day and night.

The work was nearly completed, when an order came from the Governor to seize the ship, a rumor having been widely circulated and believed, that we had a number of men on board, intending to take them to sea and enlist them, in violation of the well-established rules of International Law.

His Excellency dispatched a force of about

one hundred armed men, about half of whom belonged to the regular city police, and the rest were of the royal artillery, to enforce his order, but it is much easier to direct a party of land lubbers to seize an armed vessel than for them to execute the mandate.

Captain Waddell peremptorily refused to permit his ship to be searched, or one of the Governor's men to come on board, and in doing this, he simply stood upon his rights and dignity as the commander of a cruiser, it being contrary to all precedent, to search a man-of-war for any purpose. He also wrote to the Governor, informing him that if the ship was not released within twenty-four hours he should pay off his crew, return to England with his officers and report the outrage to his own and the English government.

An officer was dispatched with this missive, which had the desired effect.

The following day, the police and artillery were withdrawn and we were formally notified that we were at liberty to proceed to sea whenever we desired.

As an offset to this untoward little episode, an invitation came the same evening from Balarat, for our officers to attend a ball, given in their honor by a Mr. Brayton, formerly a resident of New York, but then one of the largest mining speculators of that auriferous neighbor of Melbourne.

The city of Balarat is about forty miles distant from the last named place, with which it is connected by a railway. Almost the whole of the area it occupies, has been so thoroughly perforated and undermined by shafts, sunk in pursuit of the precious ore, that if the whole town tumbled through, some fine day, it would be no matter of especial surprise to any one.

The invitation came most opportunely. After our little diplomatic escapade with the authorities we were in the mood for something in the legitimate merry-making line, and it was unanimously accepted.

As the afternoon waned, each representative of the Confederacy, dressed in his best gala trim, sallied forth, and after a pleasant railway ride of about two hours' duration, we landed at Balarat in safety, and took our way to Craig's Hotel, a most admirably conducted hostel, where the entertainment was to be given.

It was decidedly a recherché affair. The wealth, beauty, and fashion of Balarat were out in full force, fully intent upon lionizing and doing honor to a few of the unpretending supporters of a young Government battling for existence with the lusty giant of the Western world. Every attention that kindness and courtesy could suggest was shown us, and more than one heart beat quicker at such convincing evidence of the existence of sympathy in this country of the Antipodes, for the service in which we were engaged. Many a grey uniform coat lost its gilt buttons that night, but we saw them again ere we bade a final adieu to Australia, suspended from watchguards depending from the necks of bright-eyed women, and we appreciated the compliment thus paid, not to us, but to our country.

God bless the gentle women of Melbourne and Balarat! They are remembered gratefully by the officers of the renowned ship whose official history was so brief but so brilliant.

From that time forward until the end of our sojourn in Australia, it was little else than one continuous féte. Every place of public amusement was not only open to us, but our presence was earnestly solicited by the managers thereof, probably because we were curiosities, and drew well. Balls, soirées, and receptions followed in such rapid succession that the memory of one was lost in another, and, in brief, we were so persistently and continually lionized that we were in serious danger of becoming vain, and taking the glory to ourselves instead of placing it to the credit of the cause for which we labored.

Occasionally there was a little break in this delightful round of pleasures. Once I recall, a jovial party had assembled at Scott's, one of the principal hotels of Melbourne, where, if there was not a feast of reason, there was an immense flow of soul. There were perhaps fifteen or twenty collected in the large parlor, and among them a few of the officers of our ship, who were indulging in an occasional patriotic toast.

We were just sitting down to a sumptuous repast when an individual entered, invited himself to join us, and forthwith commenced a tirade upon rebels and the Southern Confederacy, making use of such language as gentlemen seldom submit to in silence.

He had not proceeded in this manner many minutes ere our Assistant Surgeon sprang to his feet, and dealt him a blow between the eyes that laid him sprawling. In another instant the fight was general; glasses and decanters were diverted from their legitimate use, and turned into missiles of offence; knives were drawn, and one or two shots were fired, but fortunately without any serious results, though for a few moments there was such a scene of excitement and confusion as I have seldom witnessed; but the Shenandoah men were victorious, drove their antagonists from the field, and then marched off to the theatre in a body, to conclude the evening in a less exhilarating pastime.

Our repairs were at length effected, and by the aid of a steam-tug, we left the slip amid the cheers of quite a concourse who had assembled to see us off, and ships were saluting in every direction as we moved along toward our former anchorage.

Before reaching it, we hauled alongside the John Frazer, a merchant ship from Liverpool, and took in three hundred tons of coal, which, with the four hundred we already had on board, gave us an ample supply for our contemplated cruise.

On the morning of the 17th of February, the steamship Great Britain arrived from England with passengers, and some astonishment was felt on board when they recognized, as some of them did, their old acquaintance, the Sea King, which should have been, according to the clearance papers she received from the London Custom House, paddling peacefully on toward Bombay, at anchor there off Melbourne, transformed into a Confederate cruiser.

The next morning about four o'clock we hove up our anchor and stood out to sea.

CHAPTER VI.

FROM MELBOURNE TO ASCENSION ISLAND.

A SURPRISE awaited us upon getting fairly outside. Our ship's company had received a mysterious addition of forty-five men, who now made their appearance from every conceivable place where a human being could conceal himself from vigilant eyes. Fourteen of the number crept out of the bowsprit, which was of iron and hollow, where they had come very near ending their existence by suffocation; twenty more turned out of some water-tanks which were dry; another detachment was unearthed from the lower hold, and at last the whole number of stowaways were mustered forward, and word was passed to the Captain to learn his pleasure concerning them.

Personally, I felt a good deal of annoyance over the affair, as it had been my watch a part of the preceding night, and strict orders had been given to prevent any sailors from coming on board except our own, as we were far from wishing to complicate ourselves in any way with the English Government. How such a number of men could have gained our decks unseen was a mystery to me then and is still; but there they were, and the question now was, how to dispose of them.

Captain Waddell soon made his appearance, not in the best of humor, and without any circumlocution demanded of our new recruits to what country they belonged and for what purpose they were there.

The old sea-dogs chuckled, rolled over their tobacco, hitched up their trousers, and with one accord, protested that they were natives of the Southern Confederacy, and had come on board thus surreptitiously for the purpose of joining us.

There was something absolutely refreshing in the effrontery with which that motley crew had first stolen on board, at the moment of our leaving port, and then claimed the privilege of remaining, on the ground that they were our countrymen. I verily believe half the nations of the earth had contributed to this proposed accession to our numbers, but sailors are genuine cosmopolitans, and, as a general thing, change their nationalities as readily as they do their names; besides we really needed their assistance, and as they had come through no connivance of ours, we determined to consider it providential, and they were all enlisted. A few who were not seamen, we made available as marines. Good men and true they proved, and very useful before our cruise was ended.

We now laid our course for New Zealand,

where we hoped to fall in with a Yankee whaler or two, but after cruising unsuccessfully for several days, we steered to the northward, and ere long sighted Drummond's Island, one of the South Pacific group, somewhat of a favorite resort of whalers, for the purpose of procuring water and fruit.

Drummond's Island is about twenty miles in circumference and lies very near the equator. As seen from the sea, its general appearance is beautiful in the extreme, and with every variety of tropical fruit growing spontaneously on its surface, and a lovely climate, tempered as it is by the breath of the great Southern Ocean, it seems too fair a spot to be the inheritance of the miserable race of savages who inhabit it. Until very recently these natives have numbered cannibalism among their accomplishments, conscientiously devouring every one whom they captured or slew in battle, and they are still among the most ferocious and degraded of the Polynesians.

When about eight miles distant from the Island, upon which we were bearing down under steam, we discovered a boat making towards us, and in about two hours it was alongside.

It contained three natives, all perfectly naked and frightfully tattooed, who brought with them an abundance of fish and fruit, which they exchanged with us for tobacco, the only article of merchandise for which they seemed disposed to barter.

We had on board an old sailor, who had visited the Island years before in an American whaler, and had acquired sufficient knowledge of their language to converse with them after a fashion. Through him we inquired of them if any whalers had been there lately, and learned that there had not within the last three months.

As there seemed no immediate prospect of capturing a prize in that vicinity, we got under way again, greatly to the astonishment of our cannibal friends, who were evidently at a loss to understand by what process we moved through the water with no sail set, or through the agency of any other motive power that they could discover. Cautiously they paddled in our wake, curiously scanning the troubled waters, beneath which the propeller was revolving, apparently with the view of studying out the mystery of the strange craft that had visited their seas, until the engineer, at a hint from the officer of the deck, performed a stirring solo upon his steam whistle, when, with every appearance of consternation, they took to their paddles, and only paused when they had placed a safe distance between themselves and the screaming monster.

Before sundown the first of the Cannibal Islands had faded in the distance, and having let our steam go down, we glided along with all sail set before the southeast trade winds, at about seven knots an hour.

The next afternoon, just before the sun disappeared below the horizon, we could discern a black speck far off to the northward. Ere long the man at the mast-head reported it to be a sail standing towards us, and before dark we brought her to by a blank cartridge from our twelve pounder. An officer was dispatched on board to ascertain her nationality, and returning, reported her to be the schooner P. Fiert of Honolulu, on a trading expedition among the islands for cocoanut oil, which is almost their sole article of merchandise.

This much of the boarding officer's report was of no especial interest, but he added an addendum that was more to the purpose. The Honolulu craft brought the gratifying intelligence that five Yankee whalers were lying at anchor off Ascension Island, so thither we steered, but made a slight detour on the way to visit Strong's Island, where whalers not unfrequently put in.

This island is situated about five hundred miles to the northward of Drummond's, and is in reality a most charming spot, so far as its physical features go. Like the one we had lately left, it produces spontaneously, all the luscious fruits of the tropical zone, and like that, also, is the abiding place of a similar degraded race, but one remove, if any, from cannibalism, the lowest depth to which humanity can fall.

About six o'clock on the afternoon of the 31st of March, we had the island on our starboard beam, and field and spy-glasses were in requisition to discover whether any sail flying the United States flag were in sight.

Steaming slowly on, we passed round the southern extremity of this ocean emerald, quite near enough to observe all its distinctive features. Plainly visible from our deck were the curious, bower-like houses where the natives shelter themselves from the torrid heat of an almost vertical sun; and stretching away behind them were little enclosures wherein were carried on their rude agricultural operations.

Viewed from the distance that we were, it seemed a very Arcadia, where man might forget the cares and turmoils of the busy world, with which the Anglo Saxon race are so characteristically familiar, and taste for himself the delights of the old pastoral days of which the poets tell us. But here, as elsewhere, "distance lent enchantment to the view," and a closer inspection would have revealed, not pastoral simplicity, but all the revolting practices of savage tribes, sunk in unregenerate barbarism.

It was dark ere we had concluded our semi-circumnavigation of the island, and as the tropical night closed around us, we could see the natives on the shore with torches in their hands, which they waved to and fro, as if to warn us of some unforeseen danger toward which we were hurrying.

There being no sail in sight we resumed our course toward Ascension Island under steam, and on the morning of April 1st, sighted land looming up several hundred feet above the level of the sea. A dense fog soon rested over the water, and fearing shoals or reefs, we stopped our engine and lay to for clearer weather.

About eight o'clock the sun shone out bright and clear, the fog slowly lifted, then gradually dispersed, and exposed to our view Ascension Island on our port bow. We immediately got up steam and stood in, and before ten o'clock a boat was observed coming out from a point of land, making directly toward us, and it was soon alongside. It proved to be a boat belonging to one of four ships, all of them with the Star Spangled Banner flying from their peaks, which we could now discern lying at anchor in a beautiful little bay, feeling as secure, no doubt, as they would have done in Boston Harbor.

The boat contained, among its other occupants, an Englishman, who had been wrecked on the island ten years before. I could scarcely conceive a more degraded looking object. He had adopted, perforce, no doubt, the habits of the Islanders; his body was tattooed with all manner of fantastic designs, and he spoke his mother tongue with hesitation and difficulty. He had married a native woman, who had borne him two children, one of whom was still living; and so far as I could learn, he was treated with kindness and considerable consideration by the savages among whom his lot had been cast, but the torrid climate, with unnatural and perhaps oftentimes disgusting food, had made sad inroads upon a naturally robust constitution, and it was plain to see that he was descending by slow but sure stages to the grave.

It appeared, from the statement of our visitors, that our ship had been mistaken by the Yankees for some vessel engaged in a coast survey, and they had good-naturedly sent out a boat with this old Englishman to pilot us safely in. Thus far we had displayed no bunting, and, as would have been naturally expected, one of the first questions our pilot asked on coming on board, was in regard to our nationality.

Not knowing in what direction his sympathies might lie, after hobnobbing as he had undoubtedly been for some days past with the crews of the United States vessels in the harbor, and fearing, in the event of his entertaining hostile sentiments, that he would run us ashore, as he might easily have done, upon a coast with which none of us were familiar; we informed him that the Shenandoah was an American man-of-war, and requested him to take us in and anchor us near the other vessels, which he readily consented to do, in consideration of the sum of thirty dollars.

He favored us with some tough old yarns touching his island experience, and if his story was to be believed, he had been often in imminent peril of life and limb from the savages, who, from first considering him in the light of material for a substantial entertainment, had at last come to regard him as a friend, and respect him as a being of superior endowments; but I doubt if anything could have induced him to return to civilized life, and indeed he was then thoroughly unfitted for it.

In the course of an hour we had ranged up within a mile of the ships, all of which we had discovered were whalers, and dropped anchor. Four boats were then lowered and manned with sailors carrying side arms and revolvers, with two officers in each boat, and when all was in readiness a blank cartridge was fired and the Confederate flag run up.

Our pilot was evidently mystified not a little at these proceedings. He stood for a few moments watching the receding boats, then turned his eyes aloft, curiously scanning the, to him, strange bunting that streamed out to the breeze, and finally, turning to the officer of the deck, he asked what flag that was, why we had fired that gun, and why those boats, filled with armed men, were putting off toward the whalers.

"All answered in a word, my hearty," responded the individual addressed. "Those four ships are prizes to the Confederate Government."

"And what the h—l is the Confederate Government?" queried the old salt, in unaffected astonishment.

"The best and biggest half of what was the United States of America. The Yankees didn't sail the Government ship to suit us, so we cut adrift and started on our own hook."

"The d—l! What are you going to do with your prizes?"

"Set them on fire by and by, after we have taken what we want out of them."

"Well, you and the Yankees must settle

that business to suit yourselves. If I had known what you were up to, maybe I should not have piloted you in, for I don't like to see a bonfire made of a good ship."

In the course of an hour our boats were seen returning, bringing with them the first and second mates of the captured whalers. The captains were not on board, having gone on shore that morning for a merry-making, little dreaming what was in store for their fleet.

We at once commenced bringing such articles as we required from the prizes, and about five o'clock in the afternoon we saw a boat putting off from the shore, which we were notified contained the festive captains.

Their astonishment may perhaps be imagined when they discovered a cruiser in that remote sea, bearing the Confederate flag. For a moment they rested on their oars as though undetermined what to do, and then put about and pulled toward the shore; but escape was not so easy. A boat was instantly dispatched in pursuit, and at the expiration of a very brief period, we had the four gentlemen on board, where their amazement was in no wise diminished in finding their officers and crews in single irons.

They bore their misfortunes, however, with as good a grace as could be expected.

A prize crew and an officer was then sent on board of each ship to take charge of it, as it was not intended to destroy them for a day or two, or at least until we had secured such stores from them as we required.

The names of the vessels captured off Ascension Island were as follows: The Edward Cary of San Francisco, the Hector of New Bedford, the Pearl of New London, and the Harvest that tried to hail from the port of Honolulu, but having no bill of transfer she was condemned with the rest.

After securing what we desired from the prizes, and giving the officers and men an opportunity of procuring such personal effects as they desired to save, the natives were allowed to go on board and ransack the doomed vessels to their hearts' content. Such a rare occasion for wholesale plundering had never occurred before, and was not likely to again, and they made the most of it. All day long they swarmed over the vessels, like driver ants upon a dead carcase, and their canoes were constantly passing to and fro, laden with ships' bread, tobacco, bits of iron, harpoons and whaling lines, and all sorts of odds and ends, until they were fairly surfeited with plundering.

On the 3d of April the work of destruction commenced. The Pearl was the first one fired, but ere the flames had gained much headway the Hector and the Edward Cary were also blazing, and the three sent forth a lurid glare which lighted up, like the eruption of a volcano, the quiet bay whose waters were disturbed by scarce a ripple, and the tropical shore far inland, with its strange vegetation and grotesque humanity; while on the strand were scattered amazed groups of natives wildly gesticulating, and evidently unable to comprehend why all this wealth should be thus ruthlessly destroyed.

The Harvest still remained intact, as she had not contributed her quota to our stores, but on the 10th she was hauled alongside, and we commenced transferring from her such articles as were suited to our need.

The next day I was specially detailed to go on shore for the purpose of formally inviting His Cannibal Majesty to visit us. As it was a state occasion, I proceeded in the Captain's gig with six good men well armed, and the old pilot to act as interpreter.

The voyage was quickly accomplished, but as we neared the beach a crowd of natives rushed down to meet us, armed with stones, which they hurl almost with the precision of a rifle-ball, and swords manufactured from sharks' teeth, the edges of which are dipped in a subtle poison that leaves certain death in any wounds they inflict. The appearance of this heathenish multitude was anything but conciliatory, and I gathered from their manner and gesticulations that they were apprehensive we had come to reclaim all or a portion of the plunder they had taken from the whalers, and were disposed to stand upon the well-known maxim that "possession is nine points of the law," and defend their booty to the last.

A few words from the interpreter explained the real object of our visit, and when they learned it was to do honor to their king that we had come, their unfriendly demonstrations subsided, though there were still two or three ferocious looking villains who eyed us askance, and I have no doubt considered what sort of roasts or barbecues we would probably make.

His Majesty was not in his customary

abiding-place, a little bamboo hut near the beach, barely large enough to contain four persons, but at a sort of Government House farther inland, where some sort of festivity was in progress. Two or three of his chiefs volunteered to escort me thither, and leaving my men in the boat and accompanied by the interpreter, I set forth for the first time in my life to pay a visit to royalty. It was more of a walk than I had anticipated, and the way led over some steep, rugged ascents, hard enough to climb under that broiling sun, but there was much to amuse me in observing the manners and habits of this strange people, and in gaining a better insight than I had before been able to do, into their domestio economy.

Once, in passing a native hut, I observed a dog with his brains beaten out, but still retaining his skin and entrails, lying by the side of a rude oven, all ready prepared for his reception, and when I returned, a few hours later, a woman sat before the still smouldering embers gnawing the hind leg of the animal, to which the hair still adhered.

In process of time I arrived at the place where the king was holding his temporary court. It was a rude, extensive building, built of bamboo, with a high peaked roof and eaves which extended nearly to the ground, and in it were assembled some three hundred of the most hideous looking human beings it was ever my fortune to behold. The most of them were armed like those we had met on the beach with stones, and bone swords, though a few of them had spears, and I am free to confess to feeling anything but comfortable, as I stood in the presence of that fiendish looking multitude, with no attendant save the demoralized Englishman who had perhaps degenerated into a worse savage than any of them. But it was too late to turn back, even had I been disposed to do so, and assuming as nonchalant an air as possible, and feeling to see that my revolver was convenient to my hand I entered the building.

His Majesty was seated on a platform raised a few inches above the floor, and on my entrance, arose to meet me. He was a miserable little savage scarcely more than five feet high, naked with the exception of a tappa made of grass, worn about his waist and smeared from head to foot with cocoanut oil. Like most of his followers, he wore thrust through a hole made in the lobe of his ear for the purpose, a huge misshapen tobacco pipe, an arrangement which, however convenient, did not add in the least to his personal appearance.

A number of his subjects were employed in making *gorwa*, a kind of intoxicating beverage manufactured from roots crushed between stones, and afterwards left to ferment; an industrial pursuit upon which he seemed to look with peculiar favor.

The old pilot presented me in due form,

and I at once made known my errand. The King listened, looked round distrustfully a few moments, and showed himself a true diplomatist, by asking by way of answer to see my sword and revolver. Having examined these to his heart's content and taken another deliberate survey of his followers, probably querying with himself meanwhile, whether they would be able to protect him against one desperate Confederate, should he feel disposed to make a prize of him, he advanced another step in our negotiations, and invited me to take a drink, and as this was a branch of diplomacy in which I had had some practice, I complied and touched my lips to the cocoanut cup containing the vilest smelling, most nauseous compound upon which a man ever attempted to get salubrious.

These formal points of court etiquette disposed of, we returned to the real business in hand, and after a little persuasion, my royal host condescended to favor me with his company, but to effectually guard himself against any machinations that might be meditated against his peace and dignity, he gave his ugly person a fresh coating of cocoanut oil, and announced himself in readiness for the proposed excursion.

Back to the beach we wended our way, the King and a few of his chiefs, and my insignificant self taking the lead, and the whole vagabond colony following at our heels.

On reaching the shore, the King was accommodated with the seat of honor in the boat, while I placed myself out of olfactory range of the peculiar perfumes belonging to him and his retinue, and ordered the men to give way.

As we glided seaward at least a hundred boats put off and followed in our wake, each containing from three to five natives, and all keeping at a respectful distance behind, out of deference to the great man who preceded them.

On reaching the ship, Captain Waddel and his first lieutenant received his copper-colored Majesty with appropriate honors, and, after a brief inspection, conducted him to the cabin, where such a collation as our barbarous tastes could furnish, was set forth for his entertainment; but the old reprobate turned up his nose at the wine, and I strongly suspect a cold roast Confederate would have been more to his liking than the unpretending viands of our steward.

But everything passed off harmoniously, and after a couple of hours' visit, during which none of his followers had attempted to come on board, though they remained close around the ship in their canoes, he took his departure, well laden with presents of old muskets, powder, small shot, and tobacco, upon excellent terms with himself and us.

During the two or three days that followed, our men were allowed to go on shore, in limited detachments at a time, and each was furnished with a small quantity of tobacco, the standing circulating medium at Ascension, and I dare say they enjoyed themselves; at all events a pretty fair percentage of them managed to return at least three sheets in the wind on *gorwa*, unless they found a better beverage, which was not unlikely, that had been smuggled ashore from one of the whalers.

There is one place of peculiar interest on this Island. It is the remains of an old fortification, in regard to which there is not even a tradition among the natives. "The oldest inhabitant" does not profess to have even an idea of when or by whom it was built; but it is certainly a relic of considerable antiquity, and whoever erected it had no contemptible knowledge of the application of mechanical powers.

Another curious circumstance is, that it is mostly composed of huge blocks of stone, some of them four or five feet square, which must have been brought from some other locality, as nothing like them is found in any other part of the island. The generally received opinion among seamen is, that it was built by some of the ancient buccaneers as a repository for their ill-gotten gains, and a place of retreat in time of danger.

On the morning of the 13th of April we paroled all the prisoners we had on board, and having removed what we desired from the Harvest, we set her on fire. The prisoners seemed to prefer being left on shore to accompanying us on our long and uncertain voyage, so after providing them with an abundance of everything in the way of ship stores, arms, and ammunition, besides their personal effects, we bade them good-by.

I should mention that this island is provided with a missionary, unexceptionable in faith and practice I should infer, as he hailed from the goodly Commonwealth of Massachusetts, so it was fair to presume that the morals of our discomfited foes would be well cared for during their stay in his diocese.

The reverend gentleman did not pay his respects to us, but he doubtless considered us unregenerate heathen, not worth saving, if indeed divine mercy was for such as we.

The same afternoon we got up our anchor and once more proceeded to sea, taking with us a number of fresh recruits who had joined us from the last prizes.

CHAPTER VII.

FROM ASCENSION ISLAND TO THE OCHOTSK SEA.

THE old pilot accompanied us outside, taking us out safely as he had taken us in, and when a good offing was obtained, he wished us a pleasant cruise, went over the side into his little boat, and we saw him no more.

We then turned our prow northward and set forth to cruise between San Francisco and Hong Kong, trusting to intercept a few of the rich merchantmen trading to those important ports.

The first of May found us fairly in the track of these traders, and the lookouts mounted to their respective perches with renewed alacrity, and swept the sea with watchful eyes, but all to no purpose. It seemed as though the merchantmen of whom we were in pursuit, must have had a premonition of our coming; at all events, they kept out of sight, and after several days' fruitless cruising, passing and repassing leagues of that great highway for ships, we concluded to stand to the northward once more. We had not had a glimpse of a sail since leaving Ascension.

As might have been expected, this state of inactivity resulted in a dull and dissatisfied condition of things on board the Shenandoah, but on a cruiser, one constantly alternates between a life of stirring excitement and absolute stupidity.

When in pursuit of a prize, all is life and animation. The rigging is filled with eager, excited faces, spy-glasses pass from hand to hand, orders are hurriedly given and instantly obeyed, and until the capture is effected, and the ship disposed of, there is little rest for any one. Then follows, perhaps, weeks of idleness, with nothing to break the tedious monotony. The watches turn out and in, yawning, the lookouts mount aloft, and sleepily throw a glance over the broad expanse of water — at seven bells, the master comes up with his sextant, to "take the sun," and work out the position of the ship, with his logarithms, — in the forecastle, tough yarns are spun by solemn visaged old sea-dogs, and at night perhaps a violin or banjo furnishes entertainment for a little knot; but with every expedient that can be resorted to, and the working of the ship, a light labor with so many hands to assist in it, the time drags wearily, and if one has not the resource of some mental occupation, it falls, in the course of time just short of unendurable.

On the morning of the 16th, the sun arose from a sky as clear and beautiful as is ever seen in these latitudes, where the Storm Spirits comparatively seldom assemble in their might, to demonstrate to man the power of Infinity, and his own weakness.

The sea was slightly ruffled by a light breeze from the northward and westward, and we were gliding along on a bowline at the rate of five or six knots an hour, but ere night closed in, some changes began to be apparent in the face of the heavens, and the barometer gave unmistakable warning that a tempest of no ordinary fury was rapidly approaching.

Before many hours it came howling down upon us, like a vengeful demon. Our good ship staggered before the first fierce gust of the hurricane, and careened over until the ends of her lower yards were drenched by the spray of the rising sea, but she righted almost immediately, shook the water from her strong wings, nodded her head as if in defiance of the storm, and was off like an arrow from a well-drawn bow.

The next morning the gale was at its

height, and we were scudding before it at the rate of eleven or twelve knots an hour, under close reefed foretop-sail and reefed foresail. Preventer braces were got aloft, hatches battened down, and so far as possible everything was done to insure our safety.

Our old boatswain, a veteran of the British navy, who for twenty years had done battle with the elements in every part of the world, exerted himself to his utmost, and on an occasion like this, there was no better man; he was a host of himself.

Still the storm continued with unabated violence, and ere long, our maintop-sail, with a report like a shotted gun, broke from the leech-ropes, and flew away before the breath of the tornado, like a boy's kite.

The officer of the deck immediately ordered the maintop-men aloft to secure such remnants of the sail as were still attached to the yards, beating the air like gigantic whips, as if to drive away any who might attempt to repair the disaster; but a new sail had to be bent, and that right speedily, desperate as the duty seemed. For a little time the scene was absolutely terrific. Slowly and painfully the sailors toiled up the shrouds, sometimes blown against them and held there with a force that rendered further progress for the time impossible. Coolly but cautiously they made their way out upon the yard that anon pointed at an abrupt angle to the heavens, and the next instant levelled its great finger at the depths below, and proceeded with consummate skill and courage to remove what remained of the tattered sail.

In an inconceivably brief period the new sail was in its place, secured and sheeted home, and was then close-reefed by means of the revolving yard.

Scarcely was this accomplished when a heavy sea came on board, filling the deck to the waist, and for the second time since setting sail from Madeira, the ports had to be knocked out, in order to free ourselves from the tremendous weight of waters.

Every one on board was literally drenched, and we had just rid the decks of that sea when another came rolling over us, carrying away with it one man, who, strange to relate, was the next moment dashed on board again by another sea, terribly frightened but otherwise uninjured.

The ship now began to roll so heavily that the royal yards were sent down on deck and secured in the fore, main, and mizzen rigging. On, on we rushed, now rising to the summit of a mountain wave, then darting with almost the velocity of light down the dark, shining declivity, while behind us the sea reared its crested head, threatening to engulf us at once and forever.

The gale continued for twelve hours, carrying us more than a hundred miles out of our course. Thousands of right whale birds, as they are known among whalers, from being always found in the vicinity of the marine monster bearing that cognomen, were hovering over the ship, as though speculating upon the position of affairs, and wondering whether we would be able to weather the tempest.

I know not why it is, but in proportion as danger menaces on shipboard, sailors habitually grow profane, and, during the continuance of that gale, which, all things considered, I think was about the most severe of any I ever encountered, an amount of swearing was done that I never heard equalled in the same length of time.

Toward night the wind abated and was succeeded by a rain which literally poured down in streams, wetting to the skin in a moment, every one who was exposed to it; but it did us the good service of beating down the tremendous sea that was running, and the next day we were again shaping our course for the Amphitrite Straits, which form the entrance to the Ochotsk Sea, and were so named in honor of the English man-of-war by whom they were discovered.

Many birds were still following us, picking up anything that was thrown overboard from the vessel; but some of the feathered tribe with which we had been familiar for some weeks had left us, and strange ones had taken their places. The albatross we had not seen since crossing the equator, and I believe he seldom extends his travels north of the line.

We were now bound for those icy regions bordering on the Arctic circle, trusting to make a raid upon the United States whaling fleet that would enrich ourselves and inflict a heavy blow upon the enemy.

I do not suppose there were half a dozen men on board, who, of their own accord would have selected that cruising ground, notwithstanding the inducements it offered; but our orders were to proceed thither, and nothing short of the probable destruction of the ship would have been regarded as an adequate excuse for not carrying them into effect.

On the 20th of May, we saw snow for the first time, in more than a year, and cold and cheerless enough it seemed, after our long sojourn in the tropics. Chests and clothes-bags were ransacked for woollen undercloth-ing, and heavy pea-jackets and overcoats were in requisition throughout the entire ship's company, the majority of whom wished we were heading for warmer seas.

The next day we got up steam for the pur-pose of passing the Amphitrite Straits, and before nightfall, the lofty, snow-clad moun-tains of Kamtschatka, as bleak and barren as the imagination could picture, were towering upon the starboard bow.

The winds sweeping down from these frozen regions, struck to the very marrow, and a cold, disagreeable fog seemed to hang perpetually over the water, while the blink of field ice in more than one direction warned us of our proximity to the Arctic circle.

About noon the lookout reported a sail in sight, but it was sometime ere any one else could distinguish it, but before three o'clock, she was distinctly made out standing toward us, and we made more sail to come up with her.

A long stretch of field ice, however, intervened between us and the stranger, which we were obliged to partially circumnavigate, ere we could reach her. We stood along close by the western margin of the field ice, until we rounded its northern point, when we showed the Russian ensign, as the most appropriate one for a vessel of our appearance to fly in those high latitudes, to which she responded by running up the Stars and Stripes.

The Russian flag was immediately lowered, and in the place of it we showed the Confederate Stars and Bars, and a blank cartridge from our twelve pounder brought her to.

An officer was then dispatched on board, who informed the Captain that his vessel was a prize to the Confederate State Steamer Shenandoah, to which he must at once proceed with his papers.

The skipper looked at him for a moment, scratched his head, laid in a fresh chew of tobacco, and then remarked as coolly as if giving the order to heave up his anchor, "Well, I s'pose I'm taken! but who on earth would have thought of seeing one of your Southern privateers up here in the Ochotsk Sea. I have heard of some of the pranks you fellows have been playing, but I supposed *I* was out of your reach."

"Why the fact of the business is, Captain," replied the officer, facetiously, "we have entered into a treaty offensive and defensive with the whales, and are up here by special agreement to disperse their mortal enemies."

"All right! my friend. I never grumble at anything I can't help, but the whales needn't owe me much of a grudge, for the Lord knows I haven't disturbed them this voyage, though I've done my part at blubber-hunting in years gone by. But it's cold talking here, come below and take something to warm your stomach, while I get my papers."

In a little time the nonchalant old Captain announced himself in readiness, and in company with our officer, came on board the Shenandoah. Shortly after, the crew, numbering about thirty all told, were brought off in their own whale boats. They were of similar timber to their commander, and one of them remarked as he came over the side, that "he had not expected to take steam home, and to tell the truth he had just as lief trust to sail," but they accepted their change of fortune with general good humor, and even single irons and confinement in the top-gallant forecastle did not seem to materially depress their spirits.

Upon the whole, they were about as plucky and sailor-like a set of fellows as fell into our hands during the entire cruise.

We remained near the prize all night, taking out such stores as suited our fancy. There was a quantity of liquor on board which the Captain had brought along, with the view of trading for furs on the coast of Siberia. This part of the whaler's cargo was soon nosed out by our forecastle gentry, and before the officers knew what was going on, a cask had been broached and the greater part of one watch were about as gloriously drunk as men well can be.

As soon as this was discovered, the inebriates were shut into the forecastle, and the more obstreperous placed in irons ; but while this discipline was progressing, the rest got wind of the captured treasure, and by the time one detachment were secured, another were in condition to receive the same polite attention we had shown their fellows. In brief, I think it was the most general and stupendous "spree" I ever witnessed. There was not a dozen sober men on board the ship except the prisoners, and had these not been ironed it might have proved a dearly bought frolic.

Some of the petty officers were as thoroughly inebriated as any of the men, and had to be confined in their quarters by sheer force. The carpenter, I recollect, twice burst out of his room, where we had attempted to imprison him, and finally we had to furnish "old Chips" with a pair of bracelets, and tie him into his bunk to cool off.

We never captured a prize that created so much excitement as this, and we never captured one of so little value. She had taken but a small quantity of oil, was a regular old tub, at least fifty years old, and, excepting the whiskey, had nothing in her of any consequence worth taking.

We removed twenty-five barrels of the extract of corn, to be used *in case of sickness*, and then set the old hulk on fire.

She was the Abigail, of New Bedford, commanded by Captain Nye, a veteran whaleman, who gained the good will of our officers by his never-failing good humor under adverse circumstances, and the shrewdness and tact he displayed upon all occasions.

We then steered toward the coast of Siberia, the well-known place of banishment for Russians criminals. They remain on this coast during the entire winter, engaged in the collection of furs, the greater part of which go to the support of the Government at St. Petersburg. No one can imagine, unless he has actually looked upon these inhospitable shores, what sufferings and privations these poor exiles endure. It was then the first of June. The thermometer stood fifteen degrees below the freezing point, and the ship from top to bottom was covered with ice; and if this was a specimen of a Siberian summer, some idea may be conceived of the severity of their winters, when, for long, dreary months no solar warmth loosens the frosty fetters that bind this God-forsaken region.

On the 4th of June we were fairly jammed in the ice. On every side of us, as far as the eye could reach, extended the field ice; and, as the ponderous floes came together, the crushed and mangled *debris* rose up into huge mounds of crystal blocks, seemingly as immovable and imperishable as the bluffs on shore. Indeed, it was impossible, while gazing off over the scene of wildness and desolation by which we were surrounded, to conceive the possibility of an avenue of escape opening through such barriers.

I recalled to mind Dr. Kane's account of the war he waged for so many months in the polar seas; of his little brigantine, beset as our ship now was, and the icy ramparts strengthening day by day until they formed a mausoleum where she still reposed; and had the season been farther advanced, I should have felt grave apprehensions for our safety. Not that I should have feared being frozen in for any great length of time in that latitude, but our ship had not been built to resist the rude shocks of Arctic ice, and as yet her powers of resistance had not been tested, consequently there was ground for fear that the tremendous pressure around her might result in serious consequences.

But a woman's temper is not more capricious than the movements of the ice in these Northern Seas. The next day a strong breeze sprang up from the southward, and before nightfall there was open water all around us, and the vast fields by which we had been confined were broken up and rapidly drifting toward the ocean.

We then laid our course toward Jonas Island, about two hundred miles distant and very near the centre of the Ochotsk Sea. This island is a favorite rendezvous for right whalers, — a sort of marine caravanserie, where they meet to talk over their luck, hold their "gams," and enjoy themselves generally. If we could reach it, the chances were ten to one of our falling in with a fleet of from fifteen to thirty sail, which could be captured without firing a shot; but the navigation was difficult, and, as I have said, our ship's capacity to resist the shocks of the drifting ice had not as yet been satisfactorily tested, and we almost hesitated to make the experiment.

That night we were jammed in the ice again, and as I lay in my berth, I could hear the huge blocks thundering and chafing against the side of the ship as though it would dash her in pieces. It was an anxious night to all on board. None of us were familiar with Arctic cruising, and consequently were to a great extent incompetent to judge of the imminence of the danger, but the hours of darkness wore away at last, without leaving us to mourn any serious accident. In a few places the copper had been chafed through, but this was about the greatest injury we had sustained, and soon after daylight the ice separated, through some unseen agency, leaving us free. But we had had enough of the route to Jonas Island, which may be a most desirable locality for whalemen and other amphibious animals who enjoy a temperature below zero, and have an affinity for ice-fields and fogs; but for my part, I would not spend six months thereabouts for all the leviathans that ever poured their oily treasures into the coffers of New Bedford.

The plain truth was, we were running too much risk in taking our cruiser through this sort of navigation for which she was never intended, and we reluctantly abandoned the idea of reaching the grand headquarters of the Ochotsk Sea whaling fleet.

We learned afterwards that had we persevered and succeeded, we should have made a splendid haul, but I, for one, do not regret it, for as the event proved, we did enough mischief that resulted in no good to any one, and much harm to many.

I had taken occasion at leisure intervals to make such inquiries as I could without exciting suspicion as to my motives, of the first mate of our last prize, a stanch old sailor, true as steel to his own Government, concerning the intricate navigation of Behring's Straits and the Arctic Sea beyond, where we knew there was a large whaling fleet upon which we would like to pounce, if the risk of getting there was not too great to counterbalance the good we might accomplish.

The old fellow never dreamed that I had any other purpose than to satisfy a seamanlike curiosity, and took great pleasure in pointing out upon the charts the dangerous places, and in giving me a general idea of the difficulties to be encountered on a cruise in that direction. The information thus obtained I of course reported to our Captain, which increased his desire to have a look at that locality; but to have attempted the voyage without a competent pilot would have been foolhardy in the extreme.

This want, however, was soon unexpectedly supplied. About this time the second mate of the Abigail began to express a desire to join us, and of course claimed to be a strong Southern sympathizer. He was a Baltimorean by birth, anything by profession, and a reprobate by nature. He had last shipped at San Francisco, where; I was informed by one of his shipmates, he had been hired to vote for Lincoln by a drink of whiskey, and he now proposed, after a little backing and filling, not only to cast in his lot with us, but to pilot the Shenandoah to the spot where the whaling fleet, which contained more than one vessel upon which he had served, was pursuing its bold, laborious calling.

It is always unpleasant, though sometimes necessary, to accept the services of the most disreputable of men, and as this was an opportunity which was not likely to occur again for securing a guide to the prize we sought, his overtures were received, and Thomas S. Manning was enrolled as ship's Corporal, and at once entered upon the discharge of his duties.

Having gone over to the Confederacy, he did nothing by halves, but set resolutely to work to induce as many as possible of his shipmates to follow his example, and several of them did so, not knowing, however, that he intended to conduct us to the ships that contained the friends and acquaintances with whom they had grown up from boyhood.

Had they been aware of it, I do not believe a man of them would have enlisted under our flag.

The remainder of the Abigail's crew stood out resolute against all inducements held out to them, and earnestly besought permission to land on the Siberian shore, from whence they imagined they could get off and join the Russian whaling fleet, cruising in the vicinity.

To this, however, Captain Waddell would not assent, and they took the disappointment philosophically, as they did the rest of their misfortunes.

The more we learned of the Abigail's crew the better we liked them, with the exception of the second mate, who, though he rendered us good service, we could not well help despising.

The old Captain developed some new phase of Yankee eccentricity every day that amused us, if it did not raise him in our estimation. Little by little it came out, partly from his own admissions and partly from the casual remarks of his officers and crew, that he was a thorough bred speculator in his own way. It was his custom, on preparing for a voyage, to lay in a quantity of cheap whiskey and second-hand clothing, which he retailed out, as opportunity offered, to his ship's company, or to the savages with whom he came in contact in the course of his cruising, at such an advance on the first cost as would have frightened a Chatham Street Jew into serious apprehensions for the future well-being of his soul.

He remarked rather gleefully to me, a day or two after the capture, that he guessed, after all, the loss of the old ship wouldn't swamp him. There was another ready for him at San Francisco as soon as he got out of our hands, and another cruise would set him all right.

I strongly suspect the old sea turtle he

commanded was insured for about her full value, and, as luck seemed to be rather against him in the whaling line, that he was more than half pleased that we had furnished him with a good market for the vessel of which he was third owner, and a free passage back to the port where he calculated on securing a better one; but of course, I wish it understood that this is merely conjecture.

We were now heading for the main land again, and soon saw it looming up in the distance. Large quantities of ice were drifting in all directions, and to save the copper from chafing, we were compelled to suspend mats made of ropes over the bows.

Having cruised in the Ochotsk Sea from the 21st of May, until the 13th of June, and only capturing one prize, we determined to lay our course for Behring's Straits, Manning acting as pilot, and evincing a thorough competency for the position.

We passed out through the same passage by which we had entered, and stood to the eastward with a moderate breeze from the southward.

CHAPTER VIII.

OUR CRUISE IN BEHRING'S STRAITS.

WE were favored with a fair wind, after losing sight of the Kamtschatkan coast, though the weather was raw and cold, and frequent fogs made navigation additionally hazardous.

We passed to the southward of Behring's Island, and came very near going ashore on its neighbor, Copper Island, in a dense fog which lifted just in time to show us our danger, and enable us to avoid it.

These islands are somewhat celebrated for the fur-bearing animals, both land and marine, that abound on them and in their vicinity. There are several varieties of seal thereabouts, which are occasionally hunted by whalers when there is a scarcity of the larger game, for the capture of which they are especially fitted out, and some foxes and brown bears are found on the islands, whose peltries excite the cupidity of the sailors, when they have nothing better to occupy their attention.

After a good passage of nine days, we sighted and stood towards Cape Thaddeus, on the coast of Asia.

This Cape is situated on the opposite meridian to Greenwich, and is usually sighted by whalers for the purpose of regulating their chronometers. It was formerly a great whaling ground and is still much frequented by vessels in that trade. A week before, thirty sail were in the vicinity, and had our visit taken place at that time, the destruction of property would have been almost incalculable.

On the 22d of June, we sighted two ships, and steamed after the nearest, which was trying out oil, as we knew by the quantity of smoke, though she was at a considerable distance.

On nearing her, an officer and a prize crew went on board and brought off the Captain and mates, from whom we learned that our prize was the William Thompson, belonging to New Bedford, and the largest whaling ship in the fleet.

Leaving the officer and prize crew in charge, we steamed after the other, and when near enough, showed the English flag, which she answered by hoisting the Stars and Stripes. We ran close alongside of her, sent an officer and prize crew on board with orders to bring off her company at once, and set the prize on fire, which was done. This was the ship Euphrates, and was also owned in New Bedford. Her crew came off to us in her own boats.

About seven o'clock P. M. we spoke the English whaler Robert Town, of Sydney,

Australia, and she was the only English vessel we saw bound for the Arctic.

We then turned round and steamed back toward the William Thompson, passing on the way the Euphrates, now one sheet of flame fore and aft. We remained in the vicinity of the first-named vessel until half past three the following morning, when that also was set on fire, and we steamed away to the northward in search of more Yankees.

The weather was excessively uncomfortable; heavy fogs were frequent, and flurries of snow not uncommon, and the quantity of floating ice we encountered somewhat impeded our progress, if it did not place us in actual peril.

About twelve o'clock at noon on the 24th, although noon and midnight were now about the same thing with us, the sun only remaining an hour or two beneath the horizon, we began to near the Behring's Straits fleet, for which we had been looking, and by four o'clock eight sail were in sight from the deck.

The sun was shining with more than its accustomed radiance as we advanced toward them, and as its rays were reflected from the glittering fields of ice, the effect was indescribably beautiful.

Away on our starboard bow we could distinguish a boat and its crew gliding swiftly through the water, towed by a large right whale to which they had just fastened, and the vessel to which it belonged was standing slowly after, to keep it in view. Other ships we could see far off in the field-ice, trying out the blubber of the ponderous animals which they pursue and capture with such consummate courage and skill; and upon the whole it was a scene of stirring activity well worth looking at.

Seals in vast numbers were swimming in the water, or composedly floating on the drifting ice, and notwithstanding their cold bed, seemed to enjoy vastly the rays of the sun that for so small a portion of the year makes its heat felt in these high latitudes.

On the starboard beam stretching away as far as the eye could reach, was a seemingly unbroken sea of ice, while on the port beam rose up the cold, dreary shores of Northern Asia, as sterile and inhospitable a region as my eyes ever looked upon.

The two vessels nearest us had foreign ensigns flying at their peaks, but the next in order sported Uncle Sam's gridiron, and all the others belonged to that same enterprising and wide-awake old gentleman.

The first that fell into our hands was the ship Milo, of New Bedford, a staunch, but slow-sailing craft, evidently built expressly for this hazardous cruising, and was well prepared to resist the drifting ice so constantly encountered in these seas. She had on board several barrels of oil, but had only just commenced whaling in earnest.

The Captain was a fine looking old veteran, standing over six feet two, and straight as an arrow. He came over the side with all the dignity of an admiral, and handed his papers to the first lieutenant who politely escorted him to the Captain's cabin.

After a brief conversation, Captain Waddell proposed to ransom the Milo for forty thousand dollars, on condition of her Captain's agreeing to take what prisoners we then had on hand, and might capture in that vicinity, to San Francisco.

He accepted the proposal readily, highly gratified, I have no doubt, at being able to save his vessel upon any terms, and the requisite bond was drawn whereby he bound his owners to pay the neat sum of forty thousand dollars at the close of the war.

I should be extremely unwilling to acquire the character of a dun, but I shall be pardoned, I trust, for reminding the parties interested that this and a number of similar vouchers taken by us during our cruise, have not yet been paid, and if they ever intend to take up these obligations, no better time than the present will ever offer. To be sure the war terminated disastrously to our cause, but we are, therefore, so much the more in need of any trifling sums that may be owing us. The above amounts, therefore, may be sent to me, care of my publisher, who is hereby authorized to receipt for the same.

When this negotiation was concluded satisfactorily to all parties, the old skipper returned on board his vessel, and dispatched his whale boats to bring off the prisoners from the Shenandoah. Several of them warmly shook hands with us at parting, and expressed the hope that we might meet again under different and more pleasing circumstances. It was a sentiment in which we could heartily concur, and I must say that American whalers are officered by some of the noblest, most high-minded and generous men belonging to the great brotherhood of seamen. A kindness they seldom forget,—to a friend their hand is ever open, and an enemy they can look upon as one who might have been a friend, but for some political accident which it is out of their line of business to examine into very closely.

While all this was transpiring, two vessels lying quite near us seemed to have awakened to the fact that the locality was a dangerous one, and to be endeavoring to arrange some plan of escape for one at least. Both were heading for the field ice, probably under the impression that while we were in pursuit of one, the other might find some opening through which we might not like to follow her, or elude us in some sudden fog, that Providence might send to her relief. All this we comprehended at a glance, and bidding the Captain of the Milo to wait and receive a farther addition to his passenger list, we got up steam and stood after the runaways.

As we approached within easy range of them, one put about and steered for the shore while the other stood boldly on into the ice. Ordering the lookout aloft to keep a sharp eye on the former, we gave our especial attention to the latter, and ranging along near the edge of the ice, we fired a shot that passed just forward of her figure head.

Still she stood on, in the desperate hope of escaping, so another shot was fired which passed through her main topsail, and being by this time convinced not only that she was within easy range but that we were capable of riddling her in a very brief period, she gave it up, went about, and steered toward our boat, which had been sent out with a prize crew as soon as we observed this last movement.

The boat was soon alongside and the officer ascended to the deck. The prize proved to be the Sophia Thornton of New Bedford, and having dispatched the Captain and his mates in one of their own boats off to us, they remained in charge, while we started in pursuit of the other, under steam and fore and aft sail, at the rate of eleven knots an hour.

Before the close of the first dog watch, we brought her to with a shot from our thirty-two pounder Whitworth rifle, which whistled past her stern. She had crowded on all the sail she could carry, but it availed her little in her laudable efforts to avoid capture.

She proved to be another New Bedforder, the Jeriah Swift, commanded by Captain Williams, a native of that city. He was said by Manning, to have about fifteen thousand dollars in specie on board, the proceeds of a quantity of oil he had lately sold, but as Captain Williams readily made oath that there was no such amount in his vessel, and we had already discovered that our newly enlisted ship's Corporal was a most accomplished liar, among his other engaging characteristics, we did not enter into a very close examination.

Within thirty minutes after the Jeriah Swift was captured, she was in flames, and having seen her crew en route for the Milo in their own boats, we were off in chase of another fellow, that, however, finally escaped into the ice.

Several of the vessels which we had first seen engaged in trying out blubber, we now discovered were surrounded by such extensive fields of ice, that we dared not venture after them, so for once these hardy voyagers, had occasion to thank as their preservers, these icy barriers that so often prove their destruction.

Captain Waddell now determined to give the prisoners permission to take whatever they desired from the Sophia Thornton, in the way of provisions and other necessaries to make them comfortable on their passage to San Francisco, so we stood back to her vicinity, where this decision was made known and was received with general satisfaction. There was an accompanying order, however, that did not meet with so much approbation. It was to fire the ship, when they had finished taking whatever they wanted away from her. This they reluctantly promised to do, but fearing, in case a favorable breeze should spring up, the temptation to run away with her would prove too strong for their virtue, we cut away the spars, and giving them to understand that they would be within range of our eight-inch shells which would certainly be dropping down among them, if our instructions were not implicitly obeyed, we again got under way.

As we glided seaward, still standing toward the frozen region of the Arctic circle, we could see the disabled vessel, with her masts dragging alongside, and the paroled prisoners in their whale boats, transferring from her to the Milo whatever suited their fancy. I have no doubt the craft was thoroughly ransacked, but ere the sun made its brief disappearance below the horizon, a bright tongue of flame shot heavenward, telling us that the prisoners had performed their distasteful task. A more unpleasant duty, I trust, will never be assigned to any of them. It is hard enough to see the oaken cradle in which one has rocked for so many weeks and months destroyed by the incendiary torch, but when necessity compels a sailor to light with his own hand the fire that is to consume the ship he has learned to love, he has good grounds for complaint against the fates, for the ungenerous usage to which they have subjected him.

The next morning we fell in with, and captured the brig Susan Abigail, a trader from San Francisco. She had a miscellaneous cargo, consisting of guns, pistols, needles, calico, twine, and Yankee notions in general, such articles in short as would be acceptable to the Esquimaux, with whom it was the Captain's intention to barter for furs.

It was a money-making trade I should judge from what I learned of it. For an old gun and some amunition, fifteen or twenty sables were freely given in exchange, and a good knife would purchase almost anything.

The Captain of the Susan Abigail when he came on board wore a magnificent fur coat, a relic of his last voyage to these seas. He begged very hard that his ship might not be burned, as that was to be his last expedition to this part of the world, and he expected to clear about thirty thousand dollars, but his eloquence was all thrown away. Captain Waddell seldom took much notice of what prisoners said, so long as his own conscience approved, and about nine o'clock, the crew having been brought off, she was set on fire. A number of men joined us from the last prize and we were now pretty thoroughly manned, thanks to the recruits we had first and last obtained from the enemy.

We then continued our course, steaming to the northward and eastward, and ere nightfall passed the burning hulk of the Sophia Thornton.

There was a heavy ice floe in sight, which necessitated the keeping of a bright lookout on board for fear of running into it. Ships, sailing in the direction we were, always keep to the westward of the ice, on account of the current which sets so strongly toward that point of the compass.

All day long the ice could be seen on our starboard beam, extending as far as the eye could reach.

About six in the evening we discovered a sail and proceeded in chase, but the fog came on so thick that we were obliged to abandon it for fear of running into some unknown danger, from which we could not extricate ourselves.

The most of the day the men had been busily engaged in killing hogs, of which we had an abundance, that had been captured with prizes. Pork must be a favorite article of diet among whalemen, at least, I do not recollect that we took a single vessel after entering the Ochotsk Sea, that did not have at least half a dozen swine on board.

We had now advanced so far north that night and day were mere arbitrary terms. For an hour or two there was a subdued twilight, or rather lack of sunshine, but at any time during the twenty-four hours there was no difficulty in reading ordinary print without the aid of artificial light.

No one can conceive until they have experienced it, the strange effect produced upon a native of the Temperate Zones by the endless day of the polar regions. There is something so supernatural and fantastic in the sight of the sun travelling perpetually round the horizon, just dipping beneath it at one point for a brief space, instead of seeing it at an angle of about sixty degrees as with us, that until you become in a measure accustomed to it, to sleep is almost an impossibility. But trying as is the long day, the long night is infinitely worse, according to the testimony of all who have experienced it.

The morning of the 21st of June found us surrounded by a fog of unusual density, and we were under the necessity of lying to in consequence. Indeed, to see a ship's length in any direction was utterly impossible, and with huge fields of ice drifting near us, and anon crashing together with a report like thunder, our situation was anything but desirable. But this is only one of the many dangers incident to Arctic sailing. It is a region of terrors, which start up grim and formidable on every side, and absolutely without an attractive feature save the wealth borne on the backs of the great right whales, or worn in the shape of choice furs by the seals that inhabit its waters, and the foxes and sables that abound upon its icy shores; and for wealth, man will dare any peril, face any danger.

Before noon the fog had cleared away, and a few hours later we sighted St. Lawrence Island, lying almost directly to the southward of Behring's Straits. It was impossible to approach very near it on account of the ice which increased in quantity as we advanced toward the Arctic Ocean. An immense field lay off our starboard bow, seemingly as impenetrable a barrier to sailing in that direction as a similar extent of solid rock.

The island is inhabited by a somewhat numerous tribe of Esquimaux, who carry on a considerable trade in furs with whalers and other vessels that visit these seas. They subsist almost exclusively upon the flesh of seals and walrus, which is generally eaten raw. How they can exist in a climate where for two months in the year the mercury freezes in the thermometer tube, is a mystery I leave others to explain.

Oh the 25th we commenced steaming, and from that time till we finally left the Arctic Seas, we made comparatively little use of our sails. An extensive ice field was ahead, and to avoid it we stood directly north.

About 10 A. M. we saw two sails on the port beam, and immediately gave chase to the nearest. She showed the Hawaiian ensign, and as her appearance corresponded with her flag, we did not intercept her, but wore around and stood after the other.

About twelve o'clock she showed the French colors, and as she did not have, on closer inspection, much of a Yankee look, we abandoned that chase also, and resumed our course to the northward and eastward.

The same afternoon we made out a sail on the starboard bow, and setting such fore and aft sail as we carried, we gave chase. We were not long in overhauling her, and, as she showed the Stars and Stripes, we passed close under her stern, within hailing distance, ordering the Captain to heave to and come on board with his papers.

The skipper took it very hard, and was quite disposed to make a personal matter of it. As he came over the side with his papers, he demanded, in a blustering, querulous manner, what injury he had ever done us, that we should hunt him like a wild animal, and destroy his property.

Of course we assured him that we had no feelings of personal animosity to gratify, that our blows were only aimed at his Government, though they might fall heavily upon private individuals; but this was far from satisfying him, and I believe, to this day, he is half inclined to the opinion that the Shenandoah went up to the Arctic expressly to look after his ship, through some spite conceived against himself by the Government of the Southern Confederacy.

This prize was the General Williams of New London, and the denizens of that wide-awake little city, must have been in a most flourishing financial condition, for she had more money on board than any vessel we captured during the entire cruise.

I pray my readers not to permit their expectations to be raised *too* high. We did not make quite so good a haul as some of the old buccaneers used to when they fell in with a Spanish ship laden with specie; but we did secure out of that New Londoner the enormous sum of four hundred dollars, and as I did not subsequently learn that any prominent New London House went down in consequence of that capture, I inferred, as above stated, that they must have enjoyed a high degree of prosperity.

While we were lying near the General Williams, we saw twenty-five or thirty boats coming off to us from St. Lawrence Island. They contained Esquimaux, who brought with them a quantity of furs and ivory, which they desired to barter for whiskey and tobacco.

Their boats were ingeniously constructed affairs. The frame is something like that of a whale boat, over which is stretched walrus hide, which renders them completely impervious to water. They are very light and much better calculated to traverse these icy seas than wood or even metallic boats.

Few and simple as their implements are, these nomadic savages succeed in capturing a good many whales. They first blow a walrus hide, previously prepared for the purpose, full of air and to this they fasten one end of their harpoon line. Watching their opportunity, they dart the harpoon into the whale, and thus attach to him a great buoy, which materially interferes with his diving propensities. Another and another is attached to him in the same way, until the poor animal can no longer get below the surface and is in the end, fairly worried to death.

We did a little trading with our Esquimaux acquaintance, and after they had taken their departure, we removed the prisoners from the General Williams, and set her on fire.

We then resumed our course, still working to the northward and eastward. A little past three P. M., three sails were reported in sight, but although a seemingly impassable barrier of ice stretched between them and our ship, we ventured into it under steam, and succeeded in passing through it safely.

At one o'clock on the morning of the 26th, we came up with them. They were the William C. Nye, the Nimrod, and the Catherine, all of New Bedford. We had little trouble in capturing these vessels. Not a breath of air was stirring, and it was of course simply impossible for them to make even an effort at escape. We already had on board about one hundred prisoners, and the officers and crews of these three prizes would have augmented the number to about two hundred and fifty, a much larger delegation of Yankees than we cared to have on board the Shenandoah at a time, with nothing to do but plot mischief; so after a little consideration, it was decided to place the last instalment of prisoners in twelve whale boats, which we took in tow.

Five more ships were now in sight, and after setting fire to the prizes we steamed after them.

It was a singular scene upon which we now looked out. Behind us were three blazing ships, wildly drifting amid gigantic fragments of ice; close astern were the twelve whale-boats with their living freight; and ahead of us the five other vessels, now evidently aware of their danger, but seeing no avenue of escape.

It was a tortuous way we now had to pursue, winding about among the ice floes like the trail of a serpent. Six knots an hour was the highest speed we dare attempt, so intricate was the navigation, but we at length succeeded in penetrating the little fleet for which we were steering.

We had learned from some of the prisoners that the small-pox prevailed on one of the vessels, and we consequently gave her a wide berth, and turned our attention to the next in order, the General Pike, of New Bedford, of which we soon made a prize. Her Captain came on board the Shenandoah, and gladly agreed to ransom his ship for thirty thousand dollars, and take our prisoners to the United States.

It required but few moments to arrange these preliminaries, and ere long our prisoners were paroled and en route for the vessel that was to take them home, and we were bearing down upon another, which proved to be the Gypsy.

It fell to my lot, as being the officer off duty, to accompany the prize crew on board of her. The Captain, who met us at the side, was terribly frightened. He was pale as a ghost, and could scarcely return an articulate answer to any question addressed to him. He evidently imagined he was to be burned with his ship, or at best run up to the yard-arm, and could scarcely believe it when I assured him that no personal injury or indignity was intended him.

His cabin was a most luxuriously fitted up affair for an Arctic whaler. There was a fine library, comprising some two hundred volumes, a beautiful writing-desk, and indeed all his furniture in style and finish would have done credit to a well-appointed drawing-room. He had also several cases of choice wines and liquors, which I destroyed to prevent the sailors from getting at them, reserving a bottle or two with which to treat my crew when they returned, after discharging the duty assigned us.

It had been the custom of the Gypsy's skipper to take his wife with him on his voyaging, but fortunately she had remained at home this cruise.

In a little time the officers and crew of the Gypsy had been paroled and transferred to the General Pike, a few furs and trinkets were appropriated, and the torch was applied.

An hour later the barque Isabel had been brought to and boarded, her crew sent off to join their countrymen, and we hauled along side of her for the purpose of filling our tanks from her water casks.

Having secured what water we wished, we steamed off a little way and set her on fire, and lay to to wait for our boat and its crew, who had performed this last duty.

As soon as they were on board we got under way, still standing to the northward.

On the 27th of June we let our fires go down, lowered our smoke-stack, and commenced beating to the northward under sail. Five ships were in sight, tacking about, little thinking what a dangerous foe was in their vicinity. The weather was cold and foggy, with a good breeze blowing, consequently we made no dash at the fleet, as a part of them would undoubtedly succeed in escaping while we were dealing with the rest. We preferred to wait for a calm when we could swoop down upon them and secure the whole.

The morning of the 28th opened with very little wind and a clear sky. It was one of the pleasantest days we experienced from the time we entered the Ochotsk Sea until we finally got clear of those icy regions. There were eight sails in sight in different directions, and land was visible on our port beam. Quantities of ice were setting to the southward and eastward, and about half past six we saw Diomede Island, about twelve miles distant.

At eight o'clock we commenced what proved to be our last day's warfare against the commerce of the United States, by starting in chase, under steam, of a sail we sighted a little way to the southward.

At ten o'clock we captured the barque Waverly, of New Bedford, with five hundred barrels of oil. Her officers and crew were at once sent on board the Shenandoah, after which she was set on fire, and we steered off to the westward until twelve o'clock and then shaped our course to the northward, passing through an extensive field of ice, and at half past one, neared a fleet of ten ships at the entrance of Behring's Straits.

For the purpose of deceiving them we hoisted the United States flag, though there was not a breath of wind at the time and not a shadow of a chance for any one of them to escape. It seemed as though the Fates had interposed to render our last achievement the most imposing and brilliant of the cruise, if not of the war.

One ship, the Brunswick, from New Bedford, had been stove, and now flew signals of distress. Under these circumstances it is the custom of whalers to collect all the vessels of the fleet within signalling distance, and, if the craft is found so badly injured that it is impossible to repair her, an auction is improvised, and she is sold to the highest bidder.

It was for such a purpose that the whaling fleet of Behring's Straits had assembled on that 28th of June, 1865, ill-omened day for them and the insurance offices of New Bedford!

Seeing our vessel standing in with the United States flag at her peak, a boat came off from the disabled Brunswick to ascertain if our Captain could lend them a carpenter or two and render any other little assistance that might be required.

We received the delegation with grave faces, and informed them that their wants should all be attended to, in due time. Our boats were then made ready for lowering, and officers and men were detailed to board the whalers and bring off their captains and mates.

When all was ready, the boats started from our ship with one accord, the United States ensign was hauled down, the Confederate run up in its place, and a blank cartridge fired toward the centre of the fleet.

All now was consternation. On every deck we could see excited groups gathering, gazing anxiously at the perfidious stranger, and then glancing wistfully aloft where their sails hung idly in the still air. But look where they would, there was no avenue of escape. The wind, so long their faithful coadjutor, had turned traitor, and left them, like stranded whales, to the mercy of the first enemy.

I said all was consternation, but that statement needs qualifying, for on board one ship, the Favorite, there was nothing of the sort. As soon as it dawned upon her grim old Captain that a wolf in sheep's clothing had strayed into their fold, he mustered his men on deck, armed them with muskets, got up his old bomb gun, an instrument made use of by some vessels to discharge the harpoon into whales, and stood resolutely on the defensive, a cutlass in one hand and an old-fashioned navy revolver in the other.

"Boat ahoy?" he bellowed, as soon as our little craft was within hailing distance.

"Ahoy!" responded the officer in charge, somewhat taken aback.

"Who are you, and what do you want?" was his next salutation.

"We come to inform you that your vessel is a prize to the Confederate Steamer Shenandoah."

"I'll be d—d if she is, at least just yet, and now keep off or I'll fire into you."

The old Spartan began to squint along his bomb gun, and the men to handle their muskets in such a decidedly business-like manner, that it was perfectly apparent that he intended to carry his threat into execution.

Seeing this, the officer in charge of the boat hailed our ship, reported the state of things, and wished to know if it was the Captain's desire that he should board her in spite of resistance.

Captain Waddell ordered the boat back to the Shenandoah, which immediately steamed towards the contumacious Yankee, and ranged alongside.

The Skipper still stood by his bomb gun with his forces drawn up on deck as though he actually meditated fighting it out.

"Haul down your flag!" shouted the officer of the deck as soon as we were near enough for his voice to be heard on board the stranger.

"Haul it down yourself! G—d d—n you!" was the plucky response, "if you think it will be good for your constitution."

"If you don't haul it down we'll blow you out of water in five minutes."

"Blow away, my buck, but may I be eternally blasted if I haul down that flag for any cussed Confederate pirate that ever floated," was the defiant rejoinder.

Captain Waddell had stood an amused spectator of this scene, and so much did he admire the old fellow's bravery, though much could not be said for his discretion, that he would not permit a shot to be fired into his ship, but dispatched an armed boat's crew to bring him off.

When he came on board, it was evident he had been seeking spirituous consolation, indeed to be plain about it, he was at least three sheets in the wind, but by general consent he was voted to be the bravest and most resolute man we captured during our cruise.

By five o'clock we had made prizes of the whole fleet, ten sail in all. One of them, the James Murray, had lost her Captain a short time previous, but his widow with her three little children were still on board.

The lady was very much frightened when the boarding officer stepped on deck and besought him, with tears in her eyes, not to destroy the ship that had been her husband's home so long.

As gently as possible he soothed her fears, telling her that no harm should befall her or the ship, through our instrumentality.

The James Murray was accordingly ransomed, and her mate was directed to take the vessel to the United States, with as many prisoners as could be conveniently accommodated.

Another of the number, the Nile, was also ransomed as a transport for the remaining prisoners, and when these had received their passengers, the remainder of the captured vessels were set on fire.

The following are the names of the vessels captured that day:

Ships Hillman, Nassau, Isaac Howland, and Brunswick. Barques Martha 2d, Congress, Waverly, and James Murray. All these belonged to New Bedford, besides the Nile of New London, and the Favorite of Fair Haven.

We hauled off to a little distance and anchored with a kedge, to watch the mighty conflagration our hands had lighted.

It was a scene never to be forgotten by any one who beheld it. The red glare from the eight burning vessels shone far and wide over the drifting ice of those savage seas; the crackling of the fire as it made its devouring way through each doomed ship, fell on the still air like upbraiding voices. The sea was filled with boats driving hither and thither, with no hand to guide them, and with yards, sails, and cordage, remnants of the stupendous ruin there progressing. In the distance, but where the light fell strong and red upon them, bringing out into bold relief each spar and line, were the two ransomed vessels, the Noah's Arks that were to bear away the human life which in a few hours would be all that was left of the gallant whaling fleet.

Imagination assisted us no doubt, but we fancied we could see the varied expressions of anger, disappointment, fear, or wonder, that marked the faces of the multitude on those decks, as their eyes rested on this last great holocaust; and when, one by one, the burning hulks went hissing and gurgling down into the treacherous bosom of the ocean, the last act in the bloody drama of the American civil war had been played. Widely different were the arenas that witnessed the opening and concluding scenes. The overture was played by the thunder of artillery beneath the walls of Sumter, with the breath of April fanning the cheeks of those who acted there their parts, while all the world looked on; the curtain finally fell amid the drifting ice of the Arctic Seas; burning vessels formed a pyrotechnic display such as the children of men have seldom looked upon, while a grim and silent cruiser, that had, even then, no government nor country, and two weather-beaten whalers, filled with despondent prisoners, were the only audience.

From one of these last prizes we obtained the first news from the States we had received for many months. She had San Francisco papers bearing date the fifteenth of April, and containing intelligence of the assassination of Abraham Lincoln.

The news occasioned a general feeling of astonishment and indignation throughout the Shenandoah. That one who sympathized with the Southern cause should have deliberately planned and executed an act that would strike with horror every honorable man, whatever his partisan sentiments might be, and thus redound to the discredit of the

Government for whose success he professed to be laboring, seemed passing strange. It was even then shadowed forth in the papers we perused so far from the place of their publication, that designing men would endeavor to fasten upon the Southern people at large, and especially upon their leaders, the odium of that hideous crime. That this has since been done, the world is well aware, but only the Southern people know how cruelly unjust is such an accusation.

It must be borne in mind that although this was the 28th of June, we had as yet received no tidings of the cessation of hostilities between the United States and the Confederacy. So far as we knew, our armies, though repulsed at many points, and sadly depleted in numbers, were still making a gallant stand against the Northern hordes, which eventually overran our unhappy country, bearing down all resistance before them; consequently our hearts were buoyed up with the thought that we were still aiding the great cause to which we had devoted our lives and fortunes.

From some source best known to himself, our pilot Manning, now advanced to the position of Acting Master's Mate, learned that a fleet comprising about sixty sail, had passed up through Behring's Straits into the Arctic Ocean, but a short time previous. Of course they were still somewhere in the ice-bound sea, from which there was no exit save the passage by which they had entered it, and we determined to overhaul them if that was possible.

At eleven o'clock P. M. we hove up our kedge and once more commenced steaming north, and by ten o'clock on the morning of the 29th we had passed through Behring's Straits, within sight, at the same time, of the extreme frontiers of Asia and North America, and were fairly within the Arctic Circle.

It was a desolate prospect that met our

view. We were at last launched on the Arctic Ocean, within whose cold embrace was clasped the prize we so much coveted; but now as far as the eye could reach, extended one vast unbroken sea of ice, where two weeks before, had been comparatively open water.

To attempt to penetrate such barriers would have been sheer madness. The undertaking would have been attended with the gravest peril, even with the auxiliary of a vessel expressly fortified and strengthened for the rough encounter, and after a brief consideration, Captain Waddell decided to make no further effort to penetrate the Polar Sea, and I do not think there was an officer or man on board who did not acquiesce in the wisdom of the decision.

The same afternoon, therefore, we put about and steamed southward, and ere the hour which should have brought nightfall, passed the burning hulks we had set on fire the preceding day, and we also had a last view of the two ships containing our prisoners, something over four hundred all told.

It was a relief to feel that we were again bound for the genial region of the tropics, our intention now being to cruise on the Pacific coast in the hopes of capturing one or more of the rich steamers that ply between San Francisco and Panama.

How others may have felt I know not, but for myself, I am free to confess, that I had had enough of Arctic cruising, and if I never look again upon those icy seas and barren shores, fit residences only for Esquimaux, seals, and Polar bears, it will not occasion me one moment's regret.

In our outward passage through the Straits, we had an illustration of the exuberance of animal life existing in these rigorous waters. Hundreds of walruses were disporting around us, now raising their huge bulks above the surface of the water and uttering their strange roaring cry, and anon disappearing beneath their native element.

We were much annoyed by the everlasting fogs prevailing in these latitudes, on our passage out, and several times were in imminent danger from this cause.

On the evening of the 30th, just as the sun was dipping below the horizon, our ship suddenly brought up all standing on a heavy cake of field ice. Officers were thrown from their berths and men from their hammocks, by the force of the concussion, and for a time the impression was general that we had struck upon a rock, and sustained serious if not fatal injury.

It was not long before we ascertained our real situation. The yards were braced back to permit the ship to go astern, while a number of men went over the side upon the floe and made lines fast by means of crowbars and kedges secured in the ice.

By such means and appliances we at last

succeeded in escaping from the dangerous locality into which we had wandered unwittingly in consequence of the fog, but it was a narrow escape, and had we not struck upon the floe, we should probably have been beset for a considerable time.

When daylight returned, a cheerless spectacle was revealed to us. Ahead of us and on both bows were great fields of floating ice extending to the utmost verge of vision, and for awhile it seemed as though we were to experience another jam, but ere long, another stretch of water opened, into which we steamed, more because it was the only space of open water than because it promised an avenue of escape, and continued our slow and painful progress southward, the ice parting before us as we advanced, as though on purpose to let our good ship through.

After four or five hours of such anxious navigation we sighted the open water again, and finally, thank God! reached it, having passed almost scathless the many perils by which we had been menaced.

The next day we passed a small island owned by the Russians, which is widely celebrated among the frequenters of these waters for the fur seals with which it abounds. It is a constant source of temptation to American whalers, who, whenever opportunity offers, organize a fillibustering expedition against these furry denizens of the far north, and the consequence is, a lively feud is generally on the *tapis* between some of them and the subjects of the Czar, who take in high dudgeon this trespass upon their hunting-ground.

We were still fairly within the right whaling-ground, and of course entertained the hope of falling in with a few more prizes before bidding a final adieu to the Arctic Seas, but in this we were disappointed. We saw no more whalers after leaving Behring's Straits, and about the 1st of July we passed out between two of the islands that form a chain running east and west, about 53° north latitude, and saw the open Pacific stretching away broad and inviting before us.

A few sheets of copper chafed off by our rude encounters was the most serious loss we had sustained.

CHAPTER IX.

THE RETURN VOYAGE TO LIVERPOOL.

THE principal part of the duty assigned us had been discharged in the destruction and dispersing of the New England whaling fleet, and it was with feelings of profound relief that we at last saw these frozen seas, with their many perils seen and unseen, where for weeks we had been battling with ice, or groping blindly in impenetrable fogs, fading in the distance.

All were in good spirits, as we had reason to be, after performing well, a laborious and in many respects unpleasant duty, and as each day carried us nearer these genial seas where for a time we expected to cruise, the memory of many hardships faded from our minds. Thus we sped us on our way.

Three weeks took us fairly into warm weather again, and never was the advent of balmy air and soft breezes hailed with more genuine delight. Heavy woollen clothing began to be no longer an indispensable concomitant of comfort, and a watch on deck instead of an irksome duty, had become a pleasant pastime. The crew were engaged in cleaning and painting the ship, and ere many days, the battered and weather-worn look she had acquired while boxing about in Arctic ice, had disappeared, and she once more assumed her old time tidiness.

We saw no sail after leaving the Straits on the 30th of June, until the 2d of August, when we sighted a barque. The wind was very light, so we got up steam, and stood toward her, flying the English ensign at our peak. As we approached, she showed the same colors, and although we had no reason to doubt from her general appearance but that she had a perfect right to carry the flag she flew, we stopped our engines and dispatched an officer on board, in the hope of obtaining some comparatively recent news from the world of which we had known so little for many weary months.

In the course of half an hour the boat returned, bringing intelligence of the gravest possible moment. The Southern cause was lost, — hopelessly — irretrievably — and the war ended. Our gallant generals, one after another, had been forced to surrender the armies they had so often led to victory. State after State had been overrun and occupied by the countless myriads of our enemies, until star by star the galaxy of our flag had faded, and the Southern Confederacy had ceased to exist.

Sadder still were the tidings that our civil Chief, who, with untiring energy and perseverance, had striven for four long, bloody years to accomplish our independence ; hopeful always when others despaired, devising some new scheme to prolong the struggle, when further resistance, to minds less clear and comprehensive than his, seemed impossible; believing in the justice of his cause, and therefore fearing not to leave the event in the hands of the God he trusted, was a captive, loaded with fetters and closely guarded in the casemate of a fortress, charged with being an accessory to the murder of Abraham Lincoln.

The news gathered from the Barracouta was as overwhelming as it was unexpected, and every man felt as though he had just learned of the death of a near and dear relative. Indeed, it is seldom that men find themselves so strangely circumstanced as we then were, and we might well feel serious apprehension.

It had been three months since hostilities ceased, leaving us without a flag or a country, and during that time we had been actively engaged in preying upon the commerce of a Government that not only claimed our allegiance, but had made good her claim by wager of battle.

It required no prophet to foretell what construction the people of the North would put upon our actions. We well knew the inveterate hatred with which they regarded the people of the seceded States. From the first they had stigmatized our cruisers as pirates, even when we were recognized as belligerents by the leading Powers of the world, and they would not be likely to let slip such an opportunity as our last escapade had furnished them with, to glut their vengeance with our blood, should we fall into their hands.

True, it would have been apparent to any unprejudiced person that cruising as we had been in the Arctic Seas, entirely out of the track of news, we could not have become cognizant, except through the interposition of a miracle, of any event transpiring in the United States, short of three or four months; but the people, who, without a shade of reason, could incarcerate Jefferson Davis, and accuse him of being implicated in a brutal murder, would not be very apt to see any extenuating circumstance in our case, and every man of us knew that if the Shenandoah was captured before she could reach an English port, that his days were numbered.

The officers of the Barracouta deeply sympathized with us in our unpleasant dilemma, but they could do nothing save wish us God-speed and a safe deliverance from the hands of our enemies; but it was very evident they entertained small hopes of our eluding the many snares that were and would be set for our feet. Several United States cruisers and one English man-of-war, they knew, had been dispatched in search of us, and it was like running a very gauntlet of life to hope to escape all these dangers unscathed.

But there was no use in repining. What had been done in the past could not be helped; the record of our deeds was written in imperishable characters, and could not be gainsaid. And now that we had no longer a country to claim our services, self-preservation was the first thing to be considered.

As soon as the English vessel had proceeded on her way, Captain Waddell summoned his whole ship's company aft, and formally announced to them the startling intelligence he had just receivcd. No man of them, he said, had any reason to blush for the service in which he had been engaged; our cruise had been projected and prosecuted in good faith; it had inflicted heavy blows upon the commerce of our late enemies, which would not soon be forgotten; but now there was nothing more to be done but to secure our personal safety by the readiest and most efficacious means at hand. As a cruiser we had no longer a right to sail the seas, for in that character we were liable to capture by the ship of any civilized nation, for we had no longer a flag to give a semblance of legality to our proceedings.

The address was listened to respectfully, and after a brief consultation among themselves, the crew presented a petition signed by nearly all of their number, requesting our Captain to proceed at once to Sydney, Australia, the nearest English port, and there abandon the ship to Her Majesty's authorities, and let each man look out for his own personal safety.

Captain Waddell at once professed to accede to this request, and for twenty-four hours the vessel was actually headed for Sydney; but events proved that he had really no intention of ever going there, and at the expiration of the time I have mentioned, he altered the course of the ship without announcing the fact to any one, and steered for Cape Horn en route for Liverpool.

From a letter of Captain Waddell's, which will be found in the latter part of this volume, it will be seen that he gives a somewhat different version of this affair, but I speak from my own personal knowledge when I say that he promised his crew to run the Shenandoah into Sydney, and then, without their cognizance, steered for another and more distant port, thus subjecting them to what they considered unnecessary peril, for the sake of securing a considerable sum of money which he knew to be lodged in the hands of one of our secret agents at Liverpool, and I farther assert that nothing like a mutinous spirit even, unless a petition they subsequently submitted may be called so, was ever manifested by any officer from the time we left the English shores till we returned to them.

It will be remembered that when we first

set sail from Madeira, the labor devolved upon us of transforming the merchantman Sea King into the cruiser Shenandoah, and now, so far as possible, that work was to be undone, and with sad hearts we betook ourselves to the task. The same tackles which had been used in transferring our armament from the Laurel to our decks, were again got aloft to assist in dismounting the heavy guns, and striking them below, beyond the reach of prying eyes — port holes were closed up, our smoke stack whitewashed, and in appearance our ship was a quiet merchantman, peacefully pursuing her way, with naught to apprehend from any vessel she might encounter on the high seas.

The hilarity which had so long been observable throughout the ship, was now gone, and there were only anxious faces to be seen in cabin, ward-room, and forecastle. The lookouts, it was true, still mounted aloft, but it was not to scan the seas for ships that might be captured, but to maintain a faithful watch and ward over any suspicious sail that might make its appearance above the horizon.

While rolling down toward the Cape, with the "brave westerlys" astern, the lookout one day reported a vessel with all sail set, to foretop-mast studding sail, standing very nearly on the same course as ourselves.

Our glasses soon revealed the fact, that she was English, and not a man-of-war, consequently there was nothing to apprehend from her, and as she seemed to bear a singular family likeness to our own good ship, we resolved to have a nearer view of her.

At the time we were under top-gallant-sails, but before many minutes the topmen were aloft loosing the royals which were soon sheeted home, and hoisted away. The fore-topmast studding sail was also broken out, and swayed aloft, the tack hauled out, the sheet sent down, and away we went to try our speed with the stranger. She seemed to understand that a race was on the *tapis*, and immediately began to show more canvas.

For a time it was doubtful how the contest would end. Both had a heavy press of sail, and were dancing along at the rate of twelve or thirteen knots an hour, but the Shenandoah was too much by the head and at last it became apparent that the stranger was slowly leaving us. Observing this we signaled her, to learn who and what she was, and the bunting soon informed us that it was the sister ship of our own, built by the same firm on the Clyde, and in brief, one was almost a counterpart of the other. It was the first time we had fallen in with a vessel that could outsail us, and had we been in equally good trim with the Englishman, I do not think either would have had an opportunity of claiming a victory.

We made a splendid run from the line to the Cape and nearly rounded it, well to the southward, without any incident worth recording, but we were not destined to get entirely clear of the Horn without a specimen of the tempestuous weather for which that locality is so widely celebrated.

We were just congratulating ourselves upon our fortunate passage round this dreaded Cape, when we encountered a gale which for a few hours was absolutely terrific, and lay to under close reefed main-topsail, and fore storm staysail, with a tarpaulin in the fore rigging to ride it out. The sea ran mountains high, dashing its spray far up into the rigging, and more than one huge wave made a clean breach over us, leaving such a quantity of water on our decks, as to engender at times grave fears for our safety. The ship was tossed about like a cockle shell, but happily we sustained no serious injury, and when the tempest had finally blown itself out we got clear of "old Cape Misery," as it is sometimes aptly called by sailors, and were once more standing on our course to the eastward, but keeping much further to the south than is ordinarily done by vessels bound for the port that we were, to avoid falling in with any cruisers that might be looking for us.

Within the next few days we passed a good many icebergs, some of them hundreds of feet in height, slowly drifting as they were influenced by the under currents of the ocean, fit representatives of the Antarctic region from whence they came.

One day we passed no less than fourteen of them. I obtained the altitude of the largest by means of the sextant, and found that from its visible base to the pinnacle, it measured no less than three hundred and twenty feet. When first discovered it bore a striking resemblance, in form, to a church with a lofty pointed spire but as we neared it and it gradually turned it assumed the appearance of a mere shapeless block of polar ice, in parts white and sparkling in the sun's rays like crystal, and in others deep blue and seemingly as imperishable as solid rock.

Of course long before this time the crew had discovered that whatever part of the world they might be steering for, they were certainly not heading for Australia, and some dissatisfaction was felt, not only by them, but by the officers, at Captain Waddell's open violation of his pledge.

Justice compels me to say that the Captain's conduct was not free from censure. He had his own reasons, as I have intimated, for preferring to reach Liverpool and there surrender his ship, but he should have announced this fact in the first place instead of promising what he did not intend to perform, and thus leading many to apprehend that he was actuated by some motive that would not bear explanation.

About this time a petition was gotten up among the officers, and signed by all of them with the exception of five, requesting the

Captain to run for Cape Town, then to the eastward of us, and there surrender the ship to the proper authorities.

To this petition he vouchsafed no response direct or otherwise. With the quartermaster he held long, confidential interviews, and to him confided his plans, which he studiously concealed from one and all of his officers, and it was only through this subaltern that we could obtain any information as to where we were bound, though of course our destination was by many suspected.

Such conduct was as injudicious as it was unjust, and gave rise to grave suspicions touching our commander's integrity of purpose, which, I am sorry to say, the event did not prove to be altogether unfounded.

At length, after several days had passed without any notice being taken of his officers' petition, he called the five who had not signed it, upon the quarter-deck, and for the first time informed them that he intended taking the ship to Liverpool.

I was one of the five. For myself, I preferred to take the chances of reaching that port where there was a probability at least that some provision had been made for us, to steering for Sydney or Cape Town, where we should have found ourselves destitute in a foreign country, whose Government, however warmly it professed to sympathize with the Confederacy in the times when she gallantly held at bay the mighty power of the United States, would have few words of welcome for the last of her adherents in this day of adversity. As in the olden time, when the wayfarer from Jerusalem to Jericho fell among thieves and was passed by by the Priest and Levite, so might we expect to receive at the hands of the world the treatment usually meted out to men who have been engaged in an enterprise that proved a failure; and if some good Samaritan met us with wine and oil, it was more than we could with reason anticipate.

But although I differed from my brother officers as to the expediency of their proposed measure, I fully agreed with them in regarding the conduct of Captain Waddell as unwarranted and ungentlemanly, and the letter he subsequently wrote denouncing them as mutineers, was one of the most dastardly returns a commander ever made to officers who from first to last had faithfully discharged every duty assigned them, and certainly never committed an act to sully their honor while on board the Shenandoah.

When about four hundred miles from the Azores, we sighted a suspicious looking sail which seemed to be lying to as though waiting for us. The wind was very light, and feeling considerable apprehension as to the stranger's character, we wore ship and stood to the southwest, getting up steam in the meantime as rapidly as possible; but that was an operation that required something like two hours, as we had been under sail ever since parting from the Barracouta.

As soon as our engines were rendered available, we furled all sail and steamed due east for about sixteen hours, making altogether a pretty wide detour. My own impression is, that she was a Yankee cruiser, and if the surmise is correct, we came near falling into the enemy's clutches, for she was only about six miles distant when first discovered.

About two weeks before our arrival in Liverpool, we were called upon to pay the last sad offices to one of our shipmates, who, just before the conclusion of that eventful voyage, launched out upon the great ocean of eternity. His name was George Canning, and he was one of those who had joined us at Melbourne, and had been promoted to be Sergeant of Marines. He represented, and we had no reason to doubt it, that he had formerly been an officer on General Polk's staff, and, while thus serving his country, had received, at the battle of Shiloh, a ball through one of his lungs, which incapacitated him for soldiering.

The wound had never entirely healed, and through it his life finally oozed away. He had been for some time unable to perform active duty, but his danger had not been considered imminent up to the very night of his death.

It so chanced that he was alone, with the exception of his attendant, an old negro, in his last moments. For an hour or more he had been lying quietly in his berth, apparently suffering little pain, when suddenly he reached forth his hand and grasped that of his sable companion.

"Good-by Weeks," he said, "I am going. Take care of yourself, old fellow;" and the next moment poor Canning was dead.

That night the body was draped for its

ocean grave in sailor fashion, by being sewn up in his own hammock, to the foot of which were securely fastened two thirty-two pound shot, and the next day the boatswain's whistle summoned "all hands to bury the dead."

A more solemnly impressive scene than a burial at sea can scarcely be imagined. At the well-known signal the whole ship's company assembled on deck, not with the gay alacrity that characterizes their movements when responding to any other summons, but with slow steps and serious faces that were in keeping with the occasion.

Upon a smooth plank, one end of which rested on the taffrail, while the other was supported by two seamen, lay the enshrouded form of our late comrade, while near by stood the ship's surgeon with open prayer-book in hand, to read the solemn Burial Service of the Roman Catholic Church, to which the deceased had been attached.

All remained uncovered while the surgeon,

with impressive voice and manner, recited the solemn formula, and as he repeated the words, "We therefore commit his body to the deep, looking for the general resurrection in the last day, when the earth and sea shall give up their dead," the inner end of the plank was lifted, and with a sullen plunge the body disappeared forever from our view.

Of Canning's antecedents we knew nothing, beyond what I have mentioned, but friends he must have had somewhere upon the face of the earth, and it must have seemed hard to die with no loved one near to minister to his last necessities.

Such, however, is too often the case with sailors, — the ocean, so long their home, in the end proves the mausoleum that takes their bodies to its keeping, and the last "good-by" is whispered in the ear of some rough but sympathetic shipmate.

Once Canning had mentioned that he had a wife living in Paris, and on our arrival in port, a notice was inserted in the public journals, mentioning his death, and inviting any relative who might see it to call at No. 11 Great George's Square, Liverpool, and receive such worldly possessions as he had left.

This death affected us all the more from its being the only one that had occurred on board the Shenandoah during her cruise, with one exception.

A poor Sandwich Islander, who had joined us from the barque Abigail, the first prize we captured in the Ochotsk Sea, died on the return passage, and far away from the sunny land of his nativity, found a sailor's grave beneath the blue water.

On the 4th of November, our reckoning showed us to be near land, and all eyes were anxiously scanning the horizon, for a glimpse of old England. We knew not what reception was in store for us, for momentous changes had taken place since we set forth on that adventurous pilgrimage round the world, but we were weary of suspense and all were desirous of making port, and learning the worst as soon as possible.

Night, however, closed around us, with nothing but the heaving sea with which we had been so long familiar, in sight, and the following morning a dense fog was hanging over the water, effectually concealing everything from view at a ship's length distance.

Extreme caution was now necessary, as we had only our chronometers and the patent log towing astern to rely upon for showing us our position, but we steamed slowly ahead with all sails furled, laying our course for St. George's Channel.

Soon the fog lifted, revealing to our view the green shores of Ireland, on our port beam, — the first land we had seen since we lost sight of the snow-clad bluffs of Northern America, one hundred and thirty-two days before.

Notwithstanding the uncertainty in which

our fate was still enshrouded, there were many happy faces to be seen on the Shenandoah's decks that memorable morning, as we glided on toward Tuska Rock Light. Soon we had that abeam, and were steaming, at the rate of nine knots an hour, to the northward and eastward toward Holyhead.

Thirteen months before, we set sail from that point in the steamer Laurel, to join our ship at Madeira, little anticipating such a return. Shipwreck, capture, and disaster in many forms, we were prepared to look forward to as things possible, but the utter collapse of our Government that had so long and so successfully stood upon the defensive, leaving our ship a veritable Ishmael of the sea, with none to claim or recognize her for other than a lawless freebooter, was such a culmination of misfortunes as none of us had counted upon. And while from full hearts more than one sincere thanksgiving, silent, but none the less acceptable perhaps, went up to Almighty God for our almost miraculous escape from those who had gone forth to hunt us, like wild beasts, to death; there was many a sorrowful association connected with this spot, where began and ended our world-renowned cruise.

CHAPTER X.

THE WELCOME WE RECEIVED FROM OUR ENGLISH FRIENDS.

AT midnight the pilot boat was seen approaching, and ere long that functionary was on board. As soon as this was known every one was on the alert, anxious to see him and learn what news he had to tell, and perhaps gain some inkling as to the spirit in which the wanderers were to be received.

As he came over the side he was met by our first lieutenant, who bade him "Good morning."

"Good morning," the pilot responded; "what ship is this?"

"The late Confederate Steamer Shenandoah."

"The deuse it is! Where have you fellows come from last?"

"From the Arctic Ocean."

"Haven't you stopped at any port since you left there?"

"No; nor been in sight of land, either. What news from the war in America?"

"It has been over so long people have got through talking about it. Jeff Davis is in Fortress Monroe, and the Yankees have had a lot of cruisers out looking for you. Haven't you seen any of them?"

"Not unless a suspicious looking craft we sighted off the Western Islands was one."

The pilot then took command of the ship which would have been received in Liverpool with so much *eclat*, had our cause triumphed in the late contest. In that event we should have been the heroes of the hour, sought after and féted as we had been at Melbourne, and crowds of visitors would have besieged us from morning till night.

But we had returned under no such auspices and our glory was departed. From no quarter did we receive a word of cordial welcome, and the journals once most clamorous for our cause, were the first to bestow upon us the epithet of "pirates," and to querulously ask why we had come there to get them into trouble with the United States. So much for the disinterested friendship of Great Britain. As long as their workshops were busy turning out arms and munitions of war for our armies in the field, and blockade runners from Southern ports were arriving at Liverpool and London, laden with the coveted cotton, they were loud in their protestations of sympathy and friendship; but when the hour of adversity came, when there was nothing more to be made out of us, these fair-weather friends coolly ignored our existence.

Before reaching the city, our pilot managed to run us aground on the bar, where we were obliged to remain until the following morning. During the night, the First Lieutenant came around and warned the officers to keep their revolvers about them, as he had seen enough to make him apprehensive that a plot was on foot among the crew to secure what valuables there were on board, and decamp. The fear that their wages would not be forthcoming, had suggested to them this desperate expedient.

It must be confessed that their prospects for payment were not brilliant; at least none but a very credulous man would feel much confidence in the feasibility of collecting a debt due him from a defunct Government.

The officers profited by the suggestion, kept their arms within reach, and maintained a vigilant watch. The crew made no demonstration, perhaps because they perceived that their plans were discovered, and that we were ready for any emergency, and possibly because sober second thought had led them to abandon a rashly-formed determination.

Soon after daylight we got clear of the bar, and steamed up the river toward the city, with the flag that had accompanied us round the world, flying at our peak for the last time. The fog shut out the town from our view, and we were not sorry for it, for we did not care to have the gaping crowd on shore witness the humiliation that was soon to befall our ship.

That afternoon we ranged astern of Her Britannic Majesty's Ship Donegal, and dropped anchor.

The First Lieutenant stood upon the poop, his arms folded on his breast, gazing at the flag under which he had so long done battle, and then turned away with tears coursing down his bronzed cheeks.

He was not alone in this exhibition of weakness, if such it was, for more than one eye, unaccustomed to weep, turned aside to conceal the unwonted drops, as at a silent signal the quartermaster hauled down the Stars and Bars, thereby surrendering the Shenandoah to the British authorities.

Sorrowfully the master rolled up the old banner, and carried it to the Captain, but he declined to encumber himself with it, so he gave it to his Secretary who was only too anxious to become its possessor.

That same afternoon the Donegal sent a prize crew on board, consisting of twenty-five marines and twenty-five sailors, who took possession of the ship and held us as prisoners until Her Majesty's pleasure concerning us was known.

Within the last year we had sent many prize crews to take possession of captured vessels, and now our turn had come to receive such an unwelcome delegation, and we appreciated better perhaps than we had ever done before, with what feelings of poignant sorrow men surrender a ship they have learned to love, and haul down a flag endeared to them by every sentiment of patriotism.

As soon as practicable, Captain Waddell delivered to the commander of the Donegal, the following letter, to be by him forwarded to Earl Russell.

"STEAMER SHENANDOAH,
November 5, 1865.

"*To the* RIGHT HON. EARL RUSSELL, *Her Britannic Majesty's Minister for Foreign Affairs:*

"I have the honor to announce to your Lordship my arrival in the waters of the Mersey, with this vessel late a ship of war in my command, belonging to the Confederate States of America.

"The singular position in which I find myself placed and the absence of all precedents on the subject, will I trust, induce your Lordship to pardon a hasty reference to a few facts connected with the cruise lately made by this ship.

"I commissioned the ship in October, 1864, under orders from the Naval Department of the Confederate States, and in pursuance of the same, commenced actively cruising against the enemy's commerce. My orders directed me to visit certain seas, in preference to others. In obedience thereto I found myself in May, June and July of this year, in the Ochotsk Sea and Arctic Ocean. Both places if not quite isolated, are still so far removed from the ordinary channels of commerce, that months would elapse before any news could reach them as to the progress or termination of the American War.

"In consequence of this awkward circumstance, I was engaged in the Arctic Ocean, in acts of war so late as the 28th of June, in ignorance of the series of reverses sustained by our arms in the field, and the obliteration of the Government under whose authority I had been acting. This intelligence I received for the first time, on communicating at sea on the 2d of August, with the British Barque Barracouta of Liverpool, fourteen days from San Francisco.

"Your Lordship can imagine my surprise at the receipt of such intelligence, and I would have given to it little consideration if an Englishman's opinion did not confirm the war news, though from an enemy's port.

"I desisted immediately from further acts of war, and determined to suspend further action, until I had communicated with a European port, where I could learn if that intelligence was true. It would not have been intelligent in me, to convey this vessel to an American port, simply because the master of the Barracouta, had said the war was ended.

"I was in an embarrassing position. I diligently examined all the law writers at my command, searching for a precedent for my guidance, in the future control, management and final disposal of the vessel. I could find none. History, is I believe, without a parallel. Finding the authority questionable, under which I considered this vessel a ship of war, I immediately discontinued cruising, and shaped my course for the Atlantic Ocean.

"As to the ship's disposal, I do not consider that I have any right to destroy her, or any further right to command her. On the contrary, I think that as all the property of the Confederate Government has reverted by the fortune of war to the Government of the United States of North America, that therefore this vessel, insomuch as it was the property of the Confederate States should accompany the other property already reverted.

"I have, therefore, sought this port as a suitable one to learn the news, and if I am without a Government, to surrender the ship, with her battery, small arms, machinery, stores, tackle and apparel complete, to Her Majesty's Government for such disposition as in its wisdom should be deemed proper.

James I. Waddell, *Commander*."

We had now to await an answer to this letter, which would advise us whether we were to be held as prisoners by the British Government, turned over to the United States authorities, or set at liberty, and there was enough in the uncertainty involving our fate to depress the most buoyant spirits. But sailors seldom quite despond. They generally discover some bright spot in the darkest horizon, and are prompt to take courage if their situation is anything short of desperate.

As night closed round us, one of the past midshipmen, with half a dozen of the junior officers at his heels, made his appearance in the steerage, and having taken the general ground that so far from having done anything to be ashamed of, we had every reason to be proud of our exploits, he proposed that care be kicked to the wall, and all apprehension drowned in a general jubilee.

It was just the kind of a proposition to strike favorably a sailor's ear, and ere long, a frolic was inaugurated that gradually extended through almost the entire ship's company. A stranger dropping down among them would have been justified in thinking, from the boisterous hilarity everywhere observable, that we had returned in triumph from some grand expedition, and were celebrating our victories; and had he been told that that noisy, rollicking company were waiting to learn whether they were to be set free or handed over to implacable enemies to be tried for their lives, he would have considered the informer either insane or endeavoring to practise upon his credulity.

The next day passed without bringing any response from Earl Russell to the Captain's communication, and among the thinking, the gravest apprehension began to be entertained. There was little else talked of among the officers, and the opinion prevailed that the British authorities, fearing that they would be held responsible for the depredations we had committed, would turn us over as a sort of peace-offering to appease the wrath of the United States, and it was tacitly understood among us that the time had arrived when each man must look out for himself.

About nine o'clock in the evening I went on deck, feeling more wretchedly depressed in spirits than I ever remember to have been before or since. A miserable, drizzly rain was falling; in brief, it was the kind of night to make one melancholy under any circumstances. I had firmly resolved that the Shenandoah and I should part company that night at all hazards. I had a constitutional objection to ornamenting the yard-arm of a Yankee man-of-war, but by the appearance of things,

I stood a remarkably fair chance of obtaining that elevated position; but how was I to effect my escape? We were at anchor in the stream, our decks were closely guarded by the marines and sailors from the Donegal, and no boat was allowed to approach us, under severe penalties.

But the attempt had to be made, — at the worst I could but fail. Approaching the marine, who was pacing backwards and forwards near where the accommodation ladder was suspended over the side, I opened a careless conversation with him, and, watching my opportunity, slipped into his hands a bottle of the veritable old whiskey we had captured in the Ochotsk Sea.

The fellow gave me an intelligent glance, pocketed his bourbon, and marched sedately forward, while I dove down to the ward room and in a few moments was completely metamorphosed into as genuine an old shell back as ever broke biscuit in a forecastle.

As I made my appearance on deck again, the sentry glanced, with a half-amused expression, at the immense sea boots, oilskin coat, and sou'wester hat which decorated my person; but his attention was conveniently called to something on the opposite side of the deck, and the next moment I was over the side and standing on the lower step of the accommodation ladder, effectually concealed from any on board, unless they were looking for me at that particular place.

A number of small boats were plying in various directions, and one of these passed so near that I was enabled to speak her without unduly elevating my voice. The man hesitated for some moments, but good nature, with perhaps the hope of a fitting pecuniary reward, finally overcame his prudence. He shot his little craft alongside. I sprang in, and in an instant was gliding shoreward.

The voyage was accomplished without accident, and ere long I set foot on the landing stage of Liverpool. I gave the boatman two pounds which left me with eight, the sole proceeds of my thirteen months' cruise in the Shenandoah.

With such feelings of relief and thankfulness as I am unable to describe, I strode along up Lime Street, in the direction of the Washington Hotel, an inn much frequented by my countrymen. As I approached it I saw Mr. Adger, a cotton speculator from Charleston, with whom I had been well acquainted, standing on the steps.

I went up to him and extended my hand. He glanced curiously at my outlandish costume, but evidently did not recognize me, which was encouraging, considering the delicate position in which I was placed, and the possible necessity of resuming a similar disguise at some future occasion, but when I told him my name, he grasped my hand with such genuine warmth, and gave me such a cordial welcome, that I felt I had indeed met a countryman.

Mr. Adger insisted upon my accompanying him to his own hotel, the Adelphi, and I complied without much persuasion. The clerks and attachés of that rather elegant establishment, stared in blank amazement when they saw Mr. Adger, whom they well knew, enter the office, yard arm and yard arm, with what seemed to be an old salt, fresh from the forecastle, and their astonishment was in no wise abated, when he demanded to have me established in the room adjoining his own.

My friend, in the kindness and generosity of his heart, would have at once supplied all my needs from his own purse, but I could not bring myself to trespass farther on his bounty, than to accept a hat which I substituted for my sou'wester, and a pair of shoes to replace my sea boots. Under my oilskin, I wore a suit of citizen's clothes, so for the time being I felt under no particular apprehension of drawing upon myself unwelcome scrutiny.

The next day I began to feel some compunctions of conscience at the way in which I had left the ship. It was true I had neither flag nor country to claim my service, but it seemed to me on reflection that it would have been more manly to have remained with my brother officers, and shared their fate, whatever it might be. The more I thought of it, the stronger became the conviction, and about ten o'clock I sallied forth from the Adelphi, firmly resolved to go on board again and take my chances with the rest.

At the landing stage, I encountered Captain North, late of the Confederate Navy, and Mr. Robinson, formerly one of our agents. On learning of my escape from and intended return to the Shenandoah, both gentlemen joined in urging me to desist from my purpose. They argued, and truly, that I could do nothing to aid my companions, many of whom had doubtless, ere this, adopted similar means of getting out of harm's way. Both were impressed with the notion that the ship's company would be transferred to the United States authorities, which simply meant resigning them to summary execution, and recommended me instead of going on board again to make a strait wake for Paris.

It required but few moments' consideration to see that this was the council of wisdom, and there did seem to be a question whether any code of honor would require me to sacrifice myself with my comrades, when all of us were powerless to aid each other.

Moodily I walked back to the hotel, revolving these things in my mind. Sometimes momentarily congratulating myself that I had acted the part of a sensible man, and again falling back upon my former opinion that it was an act of poltroonry to leave my friends in the hour of danger, whether I could render them any assistance or not.

On gaining the hotel the gratifying intelligence reached me that our troubles were soon to be over, and fortunately the rumor was ere long confirmed.

About six o'clock in the evening, Captain Paynter of the Donegal, to whom the Shenandoah had surrendered, received a telegram ordering him to at once release such of the officers and crew of that ship as were not British subjects.

As soon as he received these instructions, Captain Paynter proceeded to the Rock Ferry slip and applied for a steamboat. Mr. Thwarts, who had charge of these boats, at once placed at his disposal the steamer Bee, in which he immediately went off to our cruiser. On gaining the deck he made known the object of his visit to Captain Waddell, who ordered his officers and crew to be summoned to the quarter-deck. The roll books were brought out, and the names called in regular order. As each man answered to his name he was asked to what country he belonged, but in no instance did any acknowledge himself a British subject. The majority claimed to be either native or adopted citizens of America; but several, who insisted that they had been born in some one of the Confederate States, had an unmistakably Scotch accent, and probably opened their eyes for the first time on this world, a good deal nearer the Clyde than the Mississippi.

This formality having been gone through with, Captain Paynter informed them that they were at liberty to proceed on shore, and the intelligence was received with boisterous demonstrations of joy. Away they went forward and commenced packing up their bedding and such other articles of personal property as they possessed, which they conveyed on board the Bee, waiting to take them off to the landing stage.

When all were ready to bid a final adieu to the vessel, they collected forward and gave three lusty cheers for their late Commander, and Captain Waddell acknowledged the compliment in a brief but appropriate address. The crew then went on board the little steamer, and the last Confederate force was disbanded.

Among the many excellent and high-minded gentlemen who, first and last, during the war, acted as Confederate Agents in England, Mr. J. D. B—— stands preëminent. For the many and valuable services he rendered to his native country during the hour of her trial, he steadfastly refused to receive any compensation. A short time prior to the final collapse, several thousand pounds of the Public Fund came into his hands, which he laid aside, not knowing how else to dispose of it, to provide for the immediate necessities of such naval officers of the Confederacy as the close of the war should leave homeless and proscribed in England. Two hundred pounds from this fund was appropriated to each of the officers of the Shenandoah, as a just recompense for the long service they had rendered, and for which they could never hope to receive any other compensation.

At two different times, this fund, with directions for its disbursement, was privately conveyed to Captain Waddell after he landed in Liverpool, it being of course presumed that no more trusty custodian could be found for it.

The event proved that this confidence was shamefully abused, and a clue was at last furnished for our Commander's singular anxiety to take his ship to Liverpool instead of to Sydney or Cape Town.

Before any of his officers had learned of this provision that kindness and forethought had made for them, he summoned them to his quarters, — George's Hotel, Dale Street, Liverpool. One at a time they were admitted to his presence, and as the humor actuated him, he presented them from fifty to one hundred pounds apiece, out of the two hundred that was justly theirs. A few of his favorites, I believe, received their full bounty. The balance he coolly appropriated to himself, probably as a commission for transacting the business, nor was this the whole extent of his peculations.

The paymaster of the ship, Mr. W. Beadlove Smith, who had formerly been Secretary to the Captain of the Alabama, volunteered his services to settle with the crew, from the pay-roll in his possession, but the offer was declined, and he subsequently sent our old quartermaster Wiggins, as honest and straightforward an old sailor as ever walked a deck, to get them together and pay them from one third to one half of what was actually due them, and promise the remainder at some indefinite time in the future. For weeks after, his residence at Waterloo, a little way out of Liverpool, was besieged by these poor men clamoring for the hard-earned pittance out of which he had mercilessly defrauded them.

I may mention also, that after getting safely on shore, Captain Waddell became very solicitous to get possession of the old flag, upon which he set so little value when it was offered to him on board the Shenandoah. Its custodian declined to surrender it, whereupon the Captain had the effrontery to threaten him with the loss of his pay and bounty if it was not given up, but the man who had taken that flag to his keeping valued it far higher than pounds and pence,—the threat was indignantly disregarded, and for once, virtue was rewarded, for B—— got his money.

It is exceedingly painful for a sailor to write such things concerning a commander under whom he has served. Had Captain

Waddell been contented with simply enriching himself at the expense of those who shared the toils and perils of that cruise, which has made his name famous, I should have been silent, for the credit of the service to which I had the honor to belong, but when, after all his officers had left England, and he therefore felt secure from personal chastisement, he ventured to publish that atrocious libel concerning their honor and courage, I could not in justice to myself and my associates do less than exhibit the man to the world in his true colors.

I subjoin an extract from his letter to which I have referred, and with it close this hasty and inartistically written, but truthful narrative of the Shenandoah's *first and last cruise.*

Extract from a letter written by Captain Waddell to a gentleman in Mobile, Alabama, and dated:

"WATERLOO, NEAR LIVERPOOL,
December 27, 1865.

"I am now in exile, but far from being a ruined man. I wont go to sea any more if I can help it. The feeling shown towards me, through the restriction placed on my wife, is decided. It is just the feeling I like, though the tyranny to her is humiliating to the nature of man. I have written her to release her bondsmen, and inform the Government that she owes her allegiance to her husband. As my case now stands, I do not think the bond is worth the paper it is written upon. In a Court of law I know it would fall.

"You have seen Mr. Welles's report, I suppose. He does me justice when he writes that I ceased my depredations when I heard Mr. Davis was a prisoner. He wilfully lies when he writes that I continued cruising against the unarmed whale ships when I knew that the arms of the South had surrendered.

"The facts are these. After reaching Behring's Sea, I captured the ship William Thompson and Brig Susan Abigail. Both had left San Francisco in April last. These captures were made about the 23rd of June, and from each I received San Francisco papers. These papers professed to have the correspondence between Generals Grant and Lee concerning the surrender of Lee's army. They also stated that Mr. Davis and Cabinet were in Danville, to which the Confederate Government had been removed, and that Mr. Davis had issued a proclamation informing the Southern people that the war would be carried on with renewed vigor. I was made possessor of as late news by these two captures, as any the whalers had, and I continued my work until it was completed in the Arctic Ocean, on the 28th of June, 1865, when I had succeeded in destroying or dispersing the New England whaling fleet.

"I left the Arctic on the 29th of June, and shipped from some of the whalers eight men on that very day, — men of intelligence, all trained soldiers. It is not to be believed that these men would have taken service in the Shenandoah if they believed the war was ended.

"After leaving Behring's Sea I fell in with no vessels until I communicated with the British Barque Barracouta, from San Francisco, August 2d, fourteen days, bound for Liverpool. She informed me of the capture of Mr. Davis and a part of his Cabinet, also of the surrender of Generals Johnston's, Smith's, and Magruder's armies. The Barracouta furnished that news the first time I heard it, and I instantly ceased to cruise, and steered for Cape Horn.

"Before communicating with the Barracouta I intended to look into the Gulf of Lower California, and there await the arrival of a California steamer, bound for Panama. The Barracouta news surprised us, and among some of the officers I witnessed a terror which mortified me. I was implored to take the vessel to Australia; that to try to reach a European port would be fatal to all concerned. Petitions were signed by three fourths of the officers, asking to be taken to Cape Town, arguing and picturing the horrors of capture, and all that sort of stuff. I called the officers and crew to the quarter-deck, and said calmly to them, 'I intend taking this ship to Liverpool. I know there is risk to be run, but that has been our associate all the time. We shall be sought after in the Pacific and not in the Atlantic.'

"They supported my views, and then followed a letter from the crew, signed by seventy-one out of one hundred and ten men, saying they had confidence in me, and were willing, nay, desired to go with me wherever I thought best to take the vessel.

"I had of course a very anxious time, — painfully anxious, because the officers set a bad example to the crew. Their conduct was nothing less than mutiny. I was very decided with some of them. I had to tell one officer I would be Captain or die on the deck, and the vessel should go to no other port than Liverpool. So ended my troubles with supplications and complaints from the officers. The men behaved nobly, and stood firmly to their decision.

"When the ship was four hundred miles from the Azores, a suspicious looking vessel was seen ahead, and apparently lying to, waiting for us to come up with her. It was sunset, the wind very light, and my suspicions being aroused, I steered my course steadily until darkness closed upon us, and then I wore ship and stood southwest until steam could be gotten up, for I had not even banked fires since parting with the Barracouta. It took two hours to get steam up. When it was ready, I furled sails and stood due east for sixteen miles, and hauled on my course, steaming for one hundred miles. I believe she was a Yankee cruiser. She was only six miles off when night came on, but I evaded her successfully.

"The Shenandoah, under sail, is a sixteen-knot vessel; under steam, ten knots; — a fine sea-craft. She ran from the Arctic to Liverpool in one hundred and thirty days; from the Line on the Pacific to the Cape in twenty-six days; from the Cape to the Line on the Atlantic in twenty-six days; and from the Line to Liverpool in twenty-four days.

"Two of my crew died of disease when near Liverpool; otherwise nothing happened to mar our cruise. No accident occurred during the cruise.

"So ends my naval career, and I am called a pirate. I made New England suffer, and I do not regret it. I cannot be condemned by any honest-thinking man. I surrendered the vessel to the British Government, and all were unconditionally released. My obstinacy made enemies among some of the officers, but they now inwardly regret their action in the Cape Town affair.

"JAMES I. WADDELL."

For List of Prizes captured by the Confederate S.S. "Shenandoah," see pp. 272, 273.

LIST OF PRIZES CAPTURED BY THE CONFEDERATE S.S. "SHENANDOAH."

	Value.	Date of Capture.	From.	Bound to.	No. of Pr'sn's.
Barque Alina, of Searsport, lat. 15° 25′ N., long. 26° 44′ W........	$95,000	Oct. 30	Newport...	Buenos Ayres....	12
Schooner Charter Oak; San Francisco, lat. 7° 38′ N., long. 27° 49′ W.	15,000	Nov. 5	Boston.....	San Francisco....	9
Barque D. Godfrey, Boston, lat. 4° 42′ N., long. 28° 24′ W..........	36,000	" 8	"	Valparaiso.......	12
Brig Susan, New York, lat. 4° 24′ N., long. 26° 39′ W.............	5,436	" 10	Cardiff.....	Rio Grande......	6
S. ship Kate Prince, Portsmouth, N.H., lat. 1° 45′ N., long. 29° 22′ W.	Rsmd. 40,000	" 12	"	Bahia, S. A......	20
Schooner L. M. Stacey, Boston, lat. 1° 40′ N., long. 28° 24′ W......	15,000	" 13	Boston.....	Sandwich Islands	6
Barque Edward, whaler, N. B., lat. 37° 47′ S., long. 12° 30′ 30″ W..	20,000	Dec. 4	N. Bedford.	Whaling.........	25
" Delphine, Bangor, Me., lat. 39° 13′ S., long. 68° 33′ E......	25,000	" 29	London....	Akyab...........	17
" Adelaide, Baltimore, lat. 1° 45′ N., long. 29° 22′ W.........	B. Cargo 24,000		Baltimore..	Rio..............	15
" Pearl, New London, Ascension Island.....................	10,000	April 1	Whaling...	....	130
Edward Cary, San Francisco, "	15,000	"	" ...	....	
Ship Hector, New Bedford, "	58,000	"	" ...	....	
Barque Harvest, Honolulu, "	34,759	"	" ...	....	
" Abigail, New Bedford, Ochotsk Sea......................	16,705	May 27	" ...	....	36
Ship William Thompson, New Bedford, off Cape Thadevus........	40,925	June 22	" ...	....	35
" Euphrates, New Bedford, off Cape Thadevus................	42,320	" 22	" ...	....	35
Barque William C. Nye, New Bedford, near Behring Straits.......	31,512	" 25	" ...	....	35
Ship Sophia Thornton, " "	70,000	" 22	" ...	....	35
Barque Nimrod, " "	29,260	" 25	" ...	....	35
" Catherine, " "	26,174	" 25	" ...	....	35

" Gypsey, " "		34,369	"	25	"	... .	
" Isabella, " "		38,000	"	25	"	... .	3
" General Pike, " "	R.	30,000	"	25	"	... .	35
" Favorite, Fairhaven, near Behring Straits.................		57,896	"	28	"	... .	35
" General Williams, N. B., "		44,740	"	25	"	... .	35
" Congress, " "		55,300	"	28	"	... .	35
" Hillman, " "		33,000	"	28	"	... .	35
Ship Isaac Howland, " "		75,112	"	28	"	... .	35
Brig Susan Abigail, " "		6,500	"	25	"	... .	20
Ship Nassau, " "		40,000	"	28	"	... .	35
Barque Martha, N. B., Behring Straits............................		30,307	"	28	"	... .	35
" Waverly, " "		62,376	"	28	"	... .	35
" Covington, N. B........		30,000	"	28	"	... .	35
" Jiveh Swift, " near Behring Straits.........................		61,960	"	22	"	... .	35
Ship Brunswick, " "		16,272	"	28	"	... .	35
" James Murry, near Behring Straits............................	R.	40,550	"	28	"	... .	35
" Milo	R.	30,000	"	28	"	... .	35
Barque Nile, New London..	R.	25,550	"	28	"	... .	35
							1,053

Mrs. Mary J. Holmes' Works.

'LENA RIVERS.— . . .	A novel.	12mo. cloth,	$1.50
DARKNESS AND DAYLIGHT.— .	do.	do.	$1.50
TEMPEST AND SUNSHINE.— .	do.	do.	$1.50
MARIAN GREY.—	do.	do.	$1.50
MEADOW BROOK.—	do.	do.	$1.50
ENGLISH ORPHANS.—	do.	do.	$1.50
DORA DEANE.—	do.	do.	$1.50
COUSIN MAUDE.—	do.	do.	$1.50
HOMESTEAD ON THE HILLSIDE.—	do.	do.	$1.50
HUGH WORTHINGTON.— . . .	do.	do.	$1.50

Artemus Ward.

HIS BOOK.—The first collection of humorous writings by A. Ward. Full of comic illustrations. 12mo. cloth, $1.50

HIS TRAVELS.—A comic volume of Indian and Mormon adventures. With laughable illustrations. 12mo. cloth, $1.50

Miss Augusta J. Evans.

BEULAH.—A novel of great power. .		12mo. cloth,	$1.75
MACARIA.— do. do. .		do.	$1.75
ST. ELMO.— do. do.	*Just published.*	do.	$2.00

By the Author of "Rutledge."

RUTLEDGE.—A deeply interesting novel.		12mo. cloth,	$1.75
THE SUTHERLANDS.—	do. . .	do.	$1.75
FRANK WARRINGTON.—	do. . .	do.	$1.75
ST. PHILIP'S.— .	do. . .	do.	$1.75
LOUIE'S LAST TERM AT ST. MARY'S. . .		do.	$1.75
ROUNDHEARTS AND OTHER STORIES.—	*Just published*	do.	$1.75

Josh Billings.

HIS BOOK.—All the rich comic sayings of this celebrated humorist. With comic illustrations. . 12mo. cloth, $1.50

Mrs. Ritchie (Anna Cora Mowatt).

FAIRY FINGERS.—A capital new novel. .		12mo. cloth,	$1.75
THE MUTE SINGER.—	do. . . .	do.	$1.75
A NEW BOOK.—*In press.*	. . .	do.	$1.75

New English Novels.

BEYMINSTRE.—A very interesting novel.		12mo. cloth,	$1.75
RECOMMENDED TO MERCY.—	do. . .	do.	$1.75
TAKEN UPON TRUST.—	do. . .	do.	$1.75

Geo. W. Carleton.

OUR ARTIST IN CUBA.—A humorous volume of travels; with fifty comic illustrations by the author. 12mo. cloth, $1.50

OUR ARTIST IN PERU.— $1 50

www.ingramcontent.com/pod-product-compliance
Lightning Source LLC
LaVergne TN
LVHW010229110826
845151LV00004B/1242

* 9 7 8 1 4 2 5 5 2 5 5 3 8 *